# Teach Rocket Science, It's Way More Complex

*What's Wrong With Education and How to Fix Some of It*

# DOUG GREEN

outskirts
press

# Who is Dr. Doug Green?

Dr. Doug Green has been an educator since 1970. He taught chemistry, physics, and computer science, and worked as an administrator for thirty years at the secondary, central office, and elementary levels. He taught leadership courses for SUNY Cortland and Binghamton University and authored over 400 articles in computer and educational journals. In 2006 he retired to care for his wife who had ALS. After her death in 2009 he started DrDougGreen.com to help busy educators and parents hone their skills and knowledge. Follow him on Twitter @DrDougGreen.

# Acknowledgements

I am happy to acknowledge my wife and editor Denise Thaler Green (1951-2009). Her support was essential to any success that I enjoyed as an educator. Without her encouragement, I probably wouldn't have finished my doctorate and her continuing inspiration is a big reason that I wrote this book. I also thank my daughter Lena Green for her advice and the good people at Outskirts Press. They are real pros and I would encourage anyone considering publishing a book to give them a call.

# Table of Contents

# CHAPTER 1

# Introduction

TEACHING IS TRICKY business. If it were as easy as rocket science, which we seem to have figured out, all students would be learning as fast as their individual brains would allow. This implies that they would learn at their own individual pace, which would cause the gaps between the faster learners and the slower learners to gradually increase. In short, we know a lot more about how to make a rocket than we know about how the human brain works.

Unfortunately, our current set of reforms driven by the corporate/ political complex gives the same tests to students each year based on their born on date, regardless of their ability. It also expects teachers to close the gaps between slow and fast learners. One way to do this is to slow down the fast learners, which some schools do rather well. They can also take advantage of the ceiling effect. This results from the fact that students already scoring at or near the top have nowhere to go but down, while low scorers have lots of room for improvement. In other words, it's easier to improve if your last scores suck.

## In a Nutshell

After summarizing over 140 books and reading dozens of articles every day for my blog since my wife, Denise, died in 2009, I think I'm in a position to write a book that lives up to my lofty title. In a nutshell, the big problem with education is its one-size-fits-all nature that you still find more often than not in our schools. The main reason for this, I believe, is that the factory model that has been in place since the 19th century is convenient for the adults. It is way easier to expect all students to learn the same thing at the same time at the same pace than it is to differentiate the learning so as to make it customized for each student.

The current reform movement that gives us the test and punish culture almost forces schools to narrow the curriculum in favor of the tested subjects, math and ELA. It has pushed increased instruction of these subjects into kindergarten and pre-school and has resulted in less time spent on anything else, including recess.

It judges teachers based on test scores that are invalid for a number of reasons. This has led to just about all teachers feeling less motivated as they see their practice micro-managed by complicit administrators who are *only following orders* rather than doing what's right for children. We are also seeing more early retirements, teacher shortages, and kids being bored by endless test prep.

Reform leaders also seem to think that we have a large number of rotten teachers who need to be weeded out. While there may be a few bad apples, this number is certainly much smaller than the reformers and their lackeys in the media portray. These same non-educators must also think that there is a line of highly skilled teachers around the block waiting to take over if we can only fire more teachers.

I don't think this is true either. Unlike some countries like Finland where only top students are admitted to teacher training, just about anyone can major in education in the U.S. and on most campuses it is viewed as an easy major. Many education professors haven't managed a real-world classroom in years and student teaching experiences are way too brief.

I liken the current reform movement to Hans Christian Anderson's *The Emperor's New Clothes*. As you may recall, the emperor's advisors convinced him that his new outfit was the finest when in fact he was naked. It took a young boy in the crowd to point that out before everyone else started to believe their own eyes.

In this book, I hope to play the role of that young boy even though there are many others engaged in the same effort. Thanks to the growing movement to opt students out of state tests and creative new ways to use technology, I believe that we are on the way to something better. This book will mention some innovative practices that I think have promise.

Although I was a science teacher, I believe that I know enough about other subjects to approach them in a credible manner. I'm good at math, I'm an amateur musician, my daughter is a professional artist, my wife was an English major, I have published hundreds of articles in a variety of journals so I have a clue about writing, and Swedish is my second language. I'm a student of history, and I have exercised almost daily for the last forty years. In other words, I'm a generalist. I have also observed and evaluated teachers of every subject in kindergarten through 12th grade in my thirty plus years as an administrator.

In this book I will try to convince you that what policy-makers are promoting is wrong and I will propose what we might do to try and fix it. I will deal with as many subject areas as possible. I will draw heavily on the books I have summarized and the sites I have included in my blog. I will also draw on my personal experiences as an educator since 1970 and as a parent since 1984.

If it seems like I am trying to be controversial on purpose, I can assure you that I am. If I'm going to change anything I've got to at least get someone's attention. That is less likely to happen if I spend too much time beating around the bush. I hope you enjoy the ride and can join me in the fight for what I think our children and our dedicated educators deserve. Welcome aboard.

# CHAPTER 2

# Teaching Isn't Rocket Science; It's Way More Complex

"Despite enormous progress over the past decades, neuroscience still has not solved the really profound questions in the field." -Science Magazine Table of Contents, October 27, 2017

AT ITS CORE, rocket science is simple. You push hot gas out the back of a device and due to the conservation of momentum, the rocket goes forward. The details may be more difficult, but they are well understood and, as a result, humankind has done some pretty amazing things with rockets, not least of which is exploring space.

By contrast to the relatively simple discipline of rocket science, education is highly complex. The experimentation and application that made space travel possible is not applied to teaching and thus our collective efforts to transfer knowledge and skills to students of all ages can seem hit or miss.

While we are making some progress in understanding how people learn, we have a long way to go. Perhaps the fact that teaching programs at most, if not all, colleges are less competitive than science and engineering makes people think that teaching is easy in comparison. As teachers know, it isn't.

What makes matters worse is that promising ideas in education spread slowly, if at all, because of a resistance to change and a federally imposed standardized testing system, which stifles innovation. The field of brain research is busy and producing results that we can use in the classroom, but what we do know about the brain is far less than what we don't know.

Some findings suggest that every student should learn at her or his own pace, have some choice in what they learn, only take assessments that they are ready for, spend more time designing and making things, collaborate more often, and be judged by what they know and can do.

We know that revisiting something daily in multiple contexts aids memory as does retrieving something from memory. Problem solving is a hot topic in education, but teachers need to realize that it requires an incubation period. Ironically, distractions can aid in problem solving as they can offer helpful thoughts. Sleep also plays a vital role in problem solving.

If you have some idea about what you are going to learn, it will be easier. Try taking the final at the beginning to focus your study. These are all things we have learned from research. Unfortunately, the political class too often looks to business people for guidance when it comes to reforms. Business has the advantage of metrics that can easily tell how well it is doing. It is also under the illusion that such metrics exist in education as well. Simply put, *they don't.*

State test results are closely linked to socioeconomic status and inherited aptitudes. As such, they tend to measure what students bring to school. High-stakes tests have also narrowed and dumbed down curricula and eliminated time spent on untested subjects.

It is time everyone realized how complicated teaching is, and that one-size-fits-all teaching and testing makes things worse, not better. What we have now are governments trying hard to identify poor teachers so that they can be weeded out just as a business would weed out low performing sales staff. They do this on the assumption that there is a line of good teachers around the block ready to take their place.

As brain research moves forward, I look forward to finding out how it applies to life in the classroom. But I fear that the political and corporate class will continue to get in the way. As long as standardized tests rule what teachers do, the chance for research to be rolled out in schools diminishes, as does the chance for our students to reach the same heights as our rockets.

# References

Amrein-Beardsley, Audrey (2014). *Rethinking Value-Added Models in Education: Critical Perspective on Tests and Assessment-Based Accountability*, Routledge: New York, NY.

Carey, Benedict (2014). *How We Learn: The Surprising Truth About When, Where, and Why It Happens*, Random House: New York, NY.

Harris, Phillip, Smith, Bruce M., and Harris Joan (2011). *The Myths of Standardized Tests: Why They Don't Tell You What You Think They Do*, Rowman and Littlefeild: Lanham, MD.

# CHAPTER 3

# The Pressure On Teachers To Get Good Test Scores Makes It Inevitable They Will Cheat

"Despite the Atlanta marking scandal, teachers will still consider cheating as a means of survival." -Dr. Doug Green."

THE CHEATING SCANDAL that engulfed schools in Atlanta, Georgia, was finally settled in 2015 with criminal convictions for many involved and some teachers even being sent to prison. While the episode – dating back to 2001 – isn't the only example of cheating as a result of federally mandated testing, it is certainly the biggest to be uncovered to date.

What we don't know is how much cheating has gone on since the Federal Government started mandating high-stakes tests during the Clinton administration. The federal mandates, which continue to morph, have given schools and students an elaborate game to play, and when any system resembles a game, it's safe to say that people will try to game it.

## Pressure to Cheat

The people in Atlanta got caught because they had erasing parties where they changed answers. What they apparently didn't know was that modern scanners can pick up erasure marks and report the percentage that go from incorrect to correct.

I suspect that other schools have followed a similar path, only being much more selective about how they erase. By focusing on the kids who are on the border of passing or failing, only changing a few answers to the easiest questions the student got wrong, schools are much less likely to arouse suspicions.

Given the pressure on schools to deliver good test results, I don't doubt these are the kinds of calculations that teachers are making. Teachers – whether they go through with it or not – are now operating in a system where it is inevitable that many will at least consider cheating as a means of survival. And it is not just erasing incorrect answers. There's a whole host of other ways to cheat the system toward which teachers will increasingly be drawn.

## Gaming the System

Although some states, such as New York, are removing time constraints for tests, many others still have them. In most schools these tests take place behind closed doors containing "Do Not Disturb" signs. Tell me there are not teachers who let the timeframe slide, as no one will know.

In my view all tests should be timeless. In the real world it isn't unusual for people to stay late to get a job done rather than telling the boss that they didn't get it done on time. Teachers can also place marginal students next to top students and not aggressively proctor the action, hoping that the tendency for some students to cheat will take over.

A focus of the government on these tests is improvement from one year to the next. This may sound like a good idea, but for teachers who have many high-performing students, it's difficult to improve if scores are already near the top. If you have kids who did poorly last year, there is lots of room for improvement. In short, it's easier to improve if you suck, which provides an incentive for teachers to artificially depress scores one year so they look good the next.

Once the tests are given, there are sections that have to be graded by teachers. While teachers can't grade their own students' tests, they can give the benefit of the doubt on the tests they do grade. As a former grader I have seen this happen many times.

## What Should Teachers Do?

If I were still principal, I would tell the teachers to create interesting, engaging lessons that get the students excited about learning, and don't even think about the tests until just before they are given.

Lessons should help students internalize important knowledge and skills and use this along with new knowledge to solve problems and be creative. Also, at least three times a day make sure students get out of their seats and move around. Take them for a walk, climb some stairs, and throw in some other exercises.

One week prior to the tests, tell the students that it's time to get ready for the "testing game." Teach them how to game multiple choice questions along with any other testing tricks you have learned. Tell them it doesn't matter how well they score; they should simply do their best. No matter what happens, tell them you still love them. Remember, the first and most important thing a teacher does is develop a strong relationship with each individual student.

As for the above information about how cheating takes place, I wouldn't do anything other than give students a little extra time to finish. There are no tests in the real world, only work to be done, and I'm sure most bosses don't mind if you call a friend, poll the audience, or ask an expert.

So, teachers, operate within the rules. But, among educators, also do all you can to point out the flaws in a system that must be changed for the good of children and society. Also, if you have students whose parents want to opt them out of testing, please cooperate and don't try to talk them out of it.

CHAPTER **4**

# Are You Smarter Than Bill Gates?

"It would be very unfortunate out of this if people thought, oh, we shouldn't test students, we shouldn't test doctors, we shouldn't test drivers." -Bill Gates

IF YOU ARE reading this article, I suspect that you probably have more expertise in the field of education than Bill Gates and the other members of the corporate/political class who have given us our current test and punish reform policies. I know that I do. I've been a full-time educator since 1969. I have an earned doctorate in education theory and practice and since I retired I have much more time to stay up-to-date on educational theory and practice.

Since we may not have Bill's IQ, which at least one website claims to be 160, I need to define what I mean here by smart. Unlike Bill Gates and his wife, Malinda, I maintain that we are smart enough to know that this system is failing, while they haven't seemed to figure it out yet. In this respect, therefore, I am smarter than Bill and you probably are too.

In his book, *Outliers*, Malcolm Gladwell tells us that psychological studies have demonstrated that great artists and people with great expertise got there after putting in at least 10,000 hours of serious ef-fort and focused practice. Even Mozart didn't make great music until he hit this number.

It takes the brain this long to assimilate all that it needs to know to achieve true mastery in a field. In Bill's case, I'm sure that he had logged this amount of time in the field of computer science by the time he dropped out of Harvard. This was due to the fact that he had unprecedented access to computers from middle school on–well before personal computers were common. He, no doubt, was also highly motivated.

As for his experience in education, I doubt that he has put in his 10,000 hours studying and observing how students of all abilities think and learn. On the other hand, I have been involved in education since I started teaching in 1969. I usually worked far more than forty hours a week until I left the profession to care for my wife who had ALS. A conservative estimate would put my total hours over 80,000. During the last thirty years of my full-time work, I spent a great deal of time observing and evaluating teachers and students. As Yogi Berra once said, "You can observe a lot by watching."

Since my wife passed in 2009, I have been blogging almost every day and reading and summarizing the most salient books I can find for educators. During this period alone I have approached another 10,000 hours, and I think that these hours have been far more ben-eficial to my understanding of the field than those I logged when I worked as a full-time teacher and administrator.

In the same book, Gladwell points out that in basketball, once you get to a certain point, height stops mattering. Michael Jordan was only 6' 6". Nobel prize winners come from Harvard and Holy Cross. With IQ, once you get to about 120 you are smart enough to win a Nobel prize or make other outstanding accomplishments in the field of your choice. As many other authors have noted, hard work, focus, and determination are hallmarks of people who accomplish anything of note.

When Gwen Ifill, of the PBS News Hour, asked Gates about

parents opting kids out of tests, Bill's response was: "It would be very unfortunate out of this if people thought, oh, we shouldn't test students, we shouldn't test doctors, we shouldn't test drivers." While I agree with Bill that tests can be useful, I would remind him that not all tests and testing methods are good.

The most effective tests for learning happen when students are asked to retrieve information they have recently studied. It has been shown that efforts to retrieve what we have tried to learn are more effective than further study of the same material. I think he also knows that prompt feedback can aid learning. But does he know that students and teachers never see how they did on each question on state tests?

I recently took a test to get a motorcycle license. When I handed it in, it was graded while I watched. Had I failed, I could have studied some more and taken it again and again until I passed. I suspect doctors get prompt results as well on tests they take.

If I asked Bill if we should give tests to some students who have absolutely no chance of passing them, he might agree that this is a bad idea. Unfortunately, this is just what we are doing. Does it make sense to give the same test to all students regardless of their academic ability simply based on their date of birth? This would be like telling a high school teacher to give the same tests to their AP classes and their special education classes. All educators know this makes no sense. How come Bill and the other people driving policy don't seem to know this?

I do admire Bill and Melinda for trying to make a difference in a number of important fields such as fighting disease, poverty, and hunger. I suspect that when it comes to these fields, they rely on experts in the field for the necessary expertise. If they are doing the same in education, I would like to know which experts tell them that our current testing system makes sense.

Of course, schools and teachers should be accountable, but the policy-makers have resorted to the easy and inaccurate approach of giving everyone the same test at the same time. If I'm a parent, I want to see what my child is able to do with the help of the teacher. There are ways to assess student skills and knowledge that reflect where they truly are.

Students should be taking tests they are ready for, given immediate feedback, and offered opportunities to try again. It should be possible to see how much progress a student makes each year, but one-size-fits-all tests don't get it done in a way that informs their future learning.

We also need to admit that there is a need for subjective evaluations of student work and projects. Not everything in this world lends itself to strictly objective measurement. It should be clear to anyone with educational expertise that the evaluation of students and teachers must have a strong subjective component.

If you have access to Bill Gates or any other powerful member of the corporate/political class responsible for education policy, please encourage them to read this and to start tapping real education experts for assistance.

# References

Berra, Yogi (1998). *The Yogi Book: I Didn't Really Say Everything I said*, Workman Publishing Company, Inc: New York, NY.

The Bill and Melinda Gates Foundation: http://www.gatesfoundation.org/

Bill and Melinda Gates on the political debate over Common Core standards. PBS interview with Gwen Ifill, October 7, 2015 http://to.pbs.org/1Gk2AJG

Gladwell, Malcolm (2008). *Outliers: The Story of Success*, Little Brown and Company: New York, NY.

IQ Facts and IQ of Famous People http://bit.ly/1W7oAP5

# CHAPTER 5

# Failing At The Business Of School

"Using a business model to evaluate schools makes no sense."
-Dr. Doug Green

MANY MEMBERS OF the corporate-political class that have forced negative reforms on public education have done so thinking the schools should be run like businesses. This is no doubt a big reason for the push for one-size-fits-all standardized testing. In business it's vital to measure the quantity and quality of outputs and sales so why shouldn't schools and teachers be accountable for testing results as their lone output?

There are two big reasons why using a business model to think about education is seriously flawed:

If schools are a factory for learning, then teachers have *no control* over their raw materials. They simply take the students who walk in the front door and do what they can. This would be like Microsoft, Google, and Apple hiring random applicants and not having high standards for the quality of their raw materials, only worse.

The second reason is the *business* of school is currently run from the top by people who, for the most part, lack real expertise in the so-called business that they are running. In most districts the board is composed of elected volunteers who for the most part do not have any serious level of educational expertise. Some boards do have members who are retired educators and this may help. That's why I usually vote for them when they run. Please don't get the idea that I don't honor volunteer board members for the countless hours they put in. I hold them in great esteem.

The "raw materials" of a school business are the students. If you work in a school district with a large representation of poor and underprivileged students, English as a second language students, and special needs children, you start out with raw materials that need a lot more resources and time. Unless something fundamentally changes in those districts to provide more support to teachers and students, some teachers will get raw materials that are much more likely to achieve at a lower level on standardized tests no matter what the teachers do.

If a private or charter school has better results, it is due at least in part to the fact that it can control to some extent the raw materials. Even if students are selected by a lottery, you can't be in a lottery if you don't apply. This screens out the parents who are more neglectful or illiterate and therefore not capable of applying.

Such parents are likely to have children who would be low academic performers. Charters can also expel students who are violent and/or disruptive, who then return to the public school where they're required to be educated even if it's in an alternate school for this type of student. Regardless of where they are taught, their test scores still count.

## Business Leaders Are Not Educators and Educators Are Not Business Leaders

The people elected to school boards are mostly volunteers who get together maybe twice a month to make policy decisions that run their school districts. While some board members are former teachers or administrators, most are employed in other businesses. Even the few educators on school boards are not likely to have doctoral level expertise in the field of education.

They also might be controlled by the teachers' union who got out the vote to elect them. In most districts there is no reason why the unions can't control the school board. Turnout is usually so low that if all the teachers and their families vote, they can elect who they want.

The district superintendent may have a doctorate if the district is large enough, but most administrators do not. Due to the size of many schools and districts, administrators need to be generalists, as they have a wide range of responsibilities. Compare this to businesses where leaders at all levels generally succeed as they develop more and more specialized expertise.

Businesses also are much more likely to employ specialists where they are needed to troubleshoot problems. The problem with letting the business-elite run schools is they don't even know enough about schools to put the right experts in place or ask the right experts to troubleshoot. In short, when it comes to leadership in schools, it's *no way to run a business*.

## There's the Easy Way and the Right Way

Judging schools and teachers by tests that are unreliable and therefore invalid is easy, but bad for schools, teachers, and students. We should be seeking more advanced ways of judging the effectiveness of various teaching practices, but that is apparently more than the policy-makers can wrap their heads around.

At a time when we should be pushing toward more self-paced instruction, we focus on testing that promotes single-paced test preparation for students regardless of their ability, circumstances, or starting point. The criteria used to give tests is just the students' birth date.

## How to Get Back on Track

Now that I have explained how schools don't fit any reasonable business model, let's ask what schools can learn from businesses.

As part of my blogging effort I summarize books that I think educators and parents can use to promote learning. A significant number of these books are not education books, but books aimed at a business or the general self-improvement audience. The best example I can think of is Daniel Pink's *Drive: The Surprising Truth About What Motivates Us*.

When I was teaching, I wished that motivation was something that came in a bottle. Since it doesn't, it makes sense that educators and parents draw on this fine body of recent research on how to motivate people. I have also summarized books on how to foster creativity, which is something that schools and businesses alike seek.

A good question to the current reformers is: just how does standardized testing foster creativity or other traits businesses demand, such as the ability to collaborate? At a time when all businesses expect schools to produce creative employees, many business people promote reforms that prevent schools from doing just that.

In order to allow students to learn at their own pace, teachers have to differentiate the learning. This is difficult to do in most situations. Ironically, physical education teachers have it easy as typical students in the gym can easily perform at their current skill level and develop from there. This is just the opposite of a math class, where every student usually works on the same problem(s) at the same time.

The most promising approach in my mind is the flipped-mastery system where students watch direct instruction in small doses on their own and have classwork facilitated by the teacher. (See the Flipped chapter later in this book.) They take unit tests when they think they are ready and can retake the test after they get some help from the teacher until they master the content.

In order to shift to the model, each student needs a separate device, ideally a laptop. Many schools have already started issuing laptops to every student but most aren't there yet. The laptop also allows students to do some of their learning online, again at their own pace.

Even if your school can shift to totally self-paced learning, you will probably still have to give the standardized tests your state requires. I recommend that you just give the tests when they come along and let the students return to individualized learning when the tests are over.

I'm sure that the motivation of the business people pushing reforms is to get schools to produce better workers. While I have no problem with that, I just wish they would turn the process over to people who have the most educational expertise rather than thinking they know best. I would like to help schools produce students who will be better workers for current businesses, but many business leaders are getting in the way.

# References
Pink, Daniel. *Drive: The Surprising Truth About What Motivates Us,* Riverhead Books: New York, NY, 2011.

# CHAPTER 6

# Achievement Gaps and Ethnic Groups

"Since Hispanics have their own ethnic category, why don't French speakers? At the same time people who speak Chinese are lumped in with people from India." -Dr. Doug Green

THERE IS A lot of talk about gaps in achievement between the rich kids and poor kids, and kids from different race and ethnic groups. It should be no surprise to anyone that rich kids tend to do better in school than poor kids, and they probably always will.

Ironically, Black and Hispanic interest groups push for disaggregating test scores by race. Since the scores show gaps between Whites, Blacks, and Hispanics and between poor and non-poor kids, they reason that this should give schools incentive to try to close those gaps. I see where they're coming from, but I don't see any realistic way a school can treat kids differently due to their race and economic status.

At the center of this is the debate regarding how much one's genes and one's environment contribute to one's intelligence and one's performance in school. My favorite author on this subject, Eric Jensen, feels that the environmental side of this argument has more impact, and I fully agree.

His key book on the impact of poverty is *Teaching with Poverty in Mind: What Being Poor Does to Kids' Brains and What Schools Can Do About It*. He makes a convincing case on how the stresses that come with living in a poor home can have a negative impact on how a student performs in school. I have yet to see a convincing argument against this theory.

When it comes to minority students, I believe that they perform at lower levels in school simply because they are more likely to be poor. Translation: Whites are not smarter than Blacks and Hispanics, and Asians are not smarter than Whites. It's the varying degrees of wealth and the family conditions, along with cultural differences, that contribute to performance in school.

## Why Ethnic Categories Don't Make Sense

Another problem is where the policy-makers draw the line between racial and ethnic groups. Last time I looked, parents had to check a race box when enrolling their kids. The choices were: White, Black (not Hispanic), Hispanic, Asian, and Native American. I think some forms might allow for Multiracial, Pacific Islander, and Other categories.

Whatever the categories, they are totally arbitrary and make no sense. Worse yet is the fact that if no box is checked, either the principal has to make a determination or the clerk entering the data hits the default key, which usually makes the kid a White. As principal, I spent time turning White kids into what I thought they looked like.

Perhaps the silliest ethic group is the Hispanic category. When I say this I mean no disrespect to anyone with Hispanic heritage. To qualify here you need to simply have Spanish as your first language. I'm sure my readers know Spanish speakers of all colors who come from a wide variety of cultures. Some are very dark-skinned and some are very white.

My favorite irony is that the island where Columbus first landed, known to some as Hispaniola, is now divided into the countries of Haiti and the Dominican Republic. The Dominicans are considered

Hispanic, while the Haitians fall into the Black group. This is in spite of the fact that many Dominicans are as black as most Haitians. How is it that just because you speak a specific language, Spanish, you get your own box to check? Why don't the folks from French-speaking countries and speakers of other languages get their own boxes?

With full respect to my Black friends, the term African American also includes a wide variety of people. North of the Sahara, most of the people are Arabs. Does that mean immigrants from places like Egypt and Libya are African Americans? Head South and you find people with darker skin who have very different body types and athletic skills depending upon which coast you are near.

On the West Coast you have people who are related to American slave decedents. They have muscle types that predispose them for sprinting and jumping. For this reason, many American Blacks have distinguished themselves in sprinting and jumping at the Olympics and in other sports.

On the East Coast of Africa you have people with very dark skin who live at altitudes that give them advantages in endurance events, which require a very different muscle type. As a result, most high-level international marathons and Olympic distance races seem more like races between the all stars from Kenya and Ethiopia than worldwide competitions.

In the southern part of Africa, there are native White people who are descendants of European colonists. When these people immigrate to the United States, are they African-Americans? I've met some Whites who refer to themselves as such, but invariably do so in an attempt to be humorous.

The Asian category also has some issues. For the officials in New York, the border between Asia and Europe has been arbitrarily set on the border between Pakistan and Afghanistan. This is not exactly how most social studies teachers define the border between Europe and Asia. Many even see it as the single continent of Eurasia, which is what it looks like on the globe.

All you need to do is stand a person from India next to a person from China, for example, to understand that the Asian group doesn't make any sense either. This also means that all Afghans are considered to be White even though the country is ethnically very diverse.

## My Blacks Beat My Whites (Academically, That Is)

One year my school was one of three schools in New York where the Black kids outperformed the White kids. A research group at NYU did a study on this. Due to the pressure on schools to lower the gaps between Black and White kids I could understand why we were part of this kind of study: we had an inverse gap. At the end of the study I had to let the researchers know that my Black scores were bolstered by my Black refugees, and my White scores were lowered by a neighborhood of low functioning inbred Whites.

If you go to countries where the people qualify for refugee status and ask who would like to go to the U.S., just about every hand would go up. These countries are generally war zones and only the smart and connected get out. This is why my Black kids from Africa beat the Whites on the tests. They also had two-parent families, as single moms don't get out of war zones. Life is officially unfair.

This also explains why, from my point of view, my refugees were my best students when it came to behavior and effort. Any time one of these students stepped even a little bit out of line, all I had to do was say, "Do I have to call your parents?" Their parents all knew how important education was to their success. Thus, the children quickly adjusted their behavior.

Of the hundreds of refugees that I had as a principal from 1993 to 2006, only one family brought me a child with significant behavioral issues and complete lack of parental support. It would seem, therefore, that the system the U.S. has for vetting refugees works pretty well. That doesn't mean we shouldn't look for ways to make it better; the terrorists have said they intend to insert bad actors into the refugee stream.

## So What About the Gaps?

No matter how you measure academic progress, some students will learn faster than others. Much of this has to do with what has happened to the students at home prior to starting school. So let's assume that a school takes all the children who arrive and allows them all to learn as quickly as possible based on where they were when they arrived. The faster learners would learn faster than the kids who arrived with less parental involvement at home.

Under this ideal scenario, the gaps that existed when the kids arrived at school would *grow larger*. Any school determined to narrow the gaps, therefore, would have to slow down the faster learners; and many of our schools do just that, probably without realizing it.

For schools that still feature the traditional single pace system, the fast learner's biggest risk is boredom. For some this also leads to acting out, which can lead to discipline problems and the risk of failure. For others, school is a bit of a snooze and many learn a lot more during out of school activities.

The other way to make the gap appear to close is to allow the fast learners to bang against the learning ceiling. Thanks to the grading system in most schools, you can only get grades that are so high. With a tight upper limit, the slower students can appear to catch up as they grind into grades in the 70s and 80s while the fast learners are stuck in the 90s with nowhere to go but down.

## My Take

The key is to stop focusing on gaps and groups. Let's realize that we will always have students with a range of learning abilities and just try to see what we can do to let *every* student learn as fast as they can. If you have an idea that makes more sense let me know.

We need to look for opportunities for students to work at their own pace rather than creating one-size-fits-all lessons that are only good for students in the Goldilocks zone. Many innovative schools are working on this. If your school isn't, it's time to get started.

## References

Jensen, Eric (2009). *Teaching with Poverty in Mind: What Being Poor Does to Kids' Brains and What Schools Can Do About It* by, ACSD: Alexandria, VA.

# CHAPTER 7

# The Drive To Fire Underperforming Teachers Will Not Improve Our Schools

"When I think back to a good teacher, the thing that might have made the biggest difference, I look back and say, 'Can you really have measured that?' Therein lies the difficulty."
-Ray Rossomando, Connecticut Education Association

AS I MENTIONED, back when he was running GE, Jack Welch famously argued that leaders should fire the bottom ten percent of their workforce each year as part of an orderly continuous improvement process. Although Jack left GE in 2001, his legacy lives on in many businesses, and some think it should be applied to the teacher ranks.

In New York, each teacher must now have one independent observation by an administrator who does not work in the same school. While it may not be stated directly, the purpose is to ferret out friendly relationships between principals and teachers that some think serves to protect poor teachers.

This came to pass after the new teacher evaluation system failed to tag many teachers as ineffective. In New York 96% were rated effective or highly effective in 2015. The thinking is, if businesses can fire ten percent a year, how is it that schools only fire very few? This, of course, is complicated by tenure laws in some states that make it very difficult, time consuming, and expensive to fire a tenured teacher.

Another assumption implicit in this plan is that there is a line of better teachers around the block waiting to take the jobs of the bad teachers we fire. In fact, all states are facing teacher shortages in multiple subject areas. Unlike Finland, teachers here are not compensated well or held in generally high esteem.

Many pre-service programs are nearly open enrollment. Current reforms that feature a strong focus on standardized tests and administrative micro-management (thanks to the Common Core standards) may also be part of the reason that we are not producing enough teachers. I'm not sure I would want to go into teaching in the current environment, and I've talked to many teachers who say they retired early for the same reason.

## Bring In the Hired Gun

In bigger districts, the independent observation tasks fall to central office administrators who qualify, as they don't work in the same school. Smaller districts can resort to asking the elementary principal to observe the high school principal and vice versa. This, however, puts an additional burden on principals who may already be overburdened with daily demands.

Another option is to hire someone from the outside who is truly independent. Such observers would invariably be retired administrators like myself. This year I was hired by a small district for this purpose. I recently finished my observations of over 100 teachers and am happy to report that I didn't find any *bad* teachers. In fact, all of the teachers I observed were solid performers.

There was some variation when it came to traditional versus innovative teaching approaches. Some made effective use of technology while others didn't use it at all. What they did have in common was that they treated all students consistently with respect and in the process, developed strong working relationships.

From what I know about this district, it's clear that leadership has promoted this behavior consistently for some time. Unfortunately, this doesn't happen everywhere. The challenge most often faced was differentiating instruction and effectively and efficiently checking for understanding with daily formative assessments.

I suspect that what I discovered also applies to other schools, much to the disappointment of Governor Cuomo and his corporate donors who have much more influence than they deserve in my opinion. It seems that corporate leaders like Bill Gates and the politicians that they donate to think they know more about education than people with true expertise in the field. They don't.

I have been an educator since 1970, have an earned doctorate in educational theory and practice, and more publications than I can count. I maintain therefore, that people like me should be driving instruction rather than people who keep score by counting how many widgets they sell each quarter (See chapter 4, Are You Smarter Then Bill Gates?).

I've published other articles that suggest ways we can improve our current education system from the one-size-fits-all approach to more personalized learning (http://bit.ly/2dI0Xgf). The increased effort to find more inefficient teachers, however, isn't one of them.

I would suggest, however, that beginning administrators use experienced observers like myself to make sure they are looking for and seeing what is important. As a teacher, I didn't feel really competent until about five years into the game. I do like the idea of multiple observers, but not for the purpose of finding more incompetent teachers.

## In Comes the ESSA

According to Daarel Burnette at Education Week Online, Teacher evaluations—both their role and the mechanics of carrying them out—are a politically fraught subject, and the Every Student Succeeds Act has kicked the dust up once again as states wrestle with how to comply with teacher-quality sections of the new law.

The law requires each state to define ineffective teachers and most states have kicked that can down the road. State education officials, meanwhile, say they struggle to collect teacher quality information from districts, many of which have different evaluation systems. There are also privacy laws that in many cases prevent schools from reporting who they consider ineffective.

I agree with Ray Rossomando, the research and policy development specialist at the Connecticut Education Association, when he says: "When I think back to a good teacher, the thing that might have made the biggest difference, I look back and say, Can you really have measured that? Therein lies the difficulty."

While the corporate/political class wants hard numbers for teacher evaluation, they fail to recognize that it's something that does not lend itself totally to quantification. In other words, it will always have a significant subjective component. Sorry folks. I have been observing and evaluating teachers since 1976. Somewhere along the line, I think I became able to distinguish effective teachers from those that are ineffective.

## How Do You Spot an Effective Teacher?

So what qualities do I look for? First and foremost are the qualities of respect and relationships, which go together. Teachers who don't get that right are likely to have more than their share of discipline problems, which you can count. These are the same teachers who are most likely to self-select themselves out of the business because "spending day after day with students acting badly really sucks."

I look for teachers who appear to enjoy what they are doing, who seem passionate about teaching, and have a strong understanding of the content they teach. Students should be engaged during the lesson with only minor and immediate redirections from the teacher.

Beyond these basics come the two things that are more difficult for all teachers. They involve effective and continuous formative assessment, also known as checking for understanding, and differentiating their instruction based on these assessment results. In other words, I want to see an effort to personalize learning.

This is where I see an important role for technology. When every student has a laptop connected to the Internet, each student can be listening to different pieces of direct instruction in class, at home, on the bus, or anywhere. They would be brief videos made either by the teacher or some professional organization. They would also allow for tailored assessments that would be taken only when the student was ready and be reported to the teacher as soon as they are finished.

In addition to using their laptops for direct instruction and assessment, students should spend time getting individual or small group help from the teacher and working on individual and group projects. If I were observing teachers running this kind of classroom, it should be easy to see what the students are doing and producing. This would require some subjective opinions, but that doesn't mean that they wouldn't be more reliable and valid than the annual results from one-size-fits-all state standardized testing. For more detail on this see the chapter on flipping your class.

# References

Brown, Paul B. Should You Fire 10% of Your Employees Every Year? *Inc Online*, downloaded June 23, 2-17, http://on.inc.com/2i0kcj8.

Burnette, Daarel. States Struggle to Define 'Ineffective Teachers' Under ESSA, *Education Week Online,* May 30, 2017 http://bit.ly/2rwZ2QR.

Cross, Freddie. Teacher Shortage Areas Nationwide Listing 1990–1991 through 2016–2017, *U.S. Department of Education Office of Postsecondary Education,* August 2016, http://bit.ly/2rt5KaD.

Green, Douglas. Dr. Doug Green's Author Page, *tes,* downloaded June 23, 2017, *http://bit.ly/2dl0Xgf.*

Klein, Allison. The Every Student Succeeds Act: An Overview, *Education Week Online,* March 31, 2016. http://bit.ly/2s3SbLF .

Maghsoodnai, Mehdi. 2 Kinds of Leadership: Are You a Steve Jobs or a Jack Welch? *Inc.* Online, downloaded June 23, 2017, http://on.inc.com/2s5aW4M.

Taylor, Kate. Cuomo Fights Rating System in Which Few Teachers Are Bad, *The New York Times*, March 22, 2015, http://nyti.ms/2i0lSt0.

Tobak, Steve. 7 Employees You Should Fire, *Inc.* Online, downloaded June 23, 2017, http://on.inc.com/2s5mfdd.

# CHAPTER 8

# Why Does Special Education Have to Be Special?

"Should every child's education be special?" -Dr. Doug Green

THANKS TO THE federal Individuals with Disabilities Act, passed in 1975, students who have some kind of identifiable disability that gets in the way of keeping up with their able peers, get service from special education teachers in schools throughout the United States.

While practices vary from state to state, there is some similarity as to how these services are provided. The law is well-intentioned, and there is no doubt that much of what special education teachers do is helpful. However, we spend too much money and time on bureaucratic procedures that waste funds that could be used to pay more teachers to give more help.

The process that a child has to go through to become classified and, therefore, eligible for service creates a barrier that favors students with strong parent advocates. At the same time, it leaves some poor kids who aren't quite disabled enough out of luck.

Unlike Finland where services are provided to about half of the students at some point *before* they fall too far behind, we limit these kind of services to roughly 12% of the U.S. student population, and often wait until students are far behind their peers before we provide it.

As an elementary school principal where 90% of the students were poor, 25% were refugees, and 20% qualified for special education services, I've seen this process close up. I have great respect for the teachers involved, but found that we spent far too much time in meetings trying to determine if a given student was classifiable rather than just helping kids who seemed to need help.

## Tag 'em and Bag 'em

In order to qualify for special education services, a student needs to go through the dreaded classification process. Students who seem to need help are first referred to by a committee of teachers who try to figure out how to help the student to avoid a special ed classification. If this doesn't work, the student gets individual testing from a special education teacher and a school psychologist. When the testing is finished, the committee on special education meets to review the results and decide if a special ed classification is in order.

These meetings include the child's regular classroom teacher, a special education teacher, the school psychologist, the child's parent (if they show up, which they often didn't in my school), a parent of a student already in the special ed system, and a committee chair provided by the district. As principal, I usually attended and parents were allowed to bring in advocates and lawyers if they wished.

After about half an hour of sorting through data that almost no parent or regular ed teacher understands, it's up to the school psychologist to see if the child is eligible for one of the allowed classifications. About half of the students who make it are considered learning disabled. Other tags include the not-so-popular emotionally disturbed, cognitively challenged (formerly mentally retarded), speech impaired, and autistic. Then there is that wonderful grab bag classification called "other health impaired." This is probably overused, as it's relatively easy for parents to swallow since it just sounds like the child has some sort of illness that might go away. This is where the ADHD crowd usually gets placed.

Students whose test results fall just above the classification lines, are basically returned to their regular classes to continue floundering. Some schools will allow the special education teachers to help these kids, but in many other situations, the special ed staff is too busy dealing with classified kids to do much.

I refer to these students as "crack" kids since they are in the cracks that contain students who can't keep up with their classmates, but aren't disabled enough to qualify for significant additional help. This doesn't happen in Finland and shouldn't happen here.

## Who Called My Kid a Retard?

When non-school people hear that a school has a psychologist, they might think that such persons provide psychological services to needy students. This is not something they do with most of their time. Most of their time is devoted to individual testing for students who have been identified, retesting students who have been in the program for a while, and sitting through endless committees of special education meetings.

Let me know if you find anyone familiar with the program who doesn't think their time could be better spent. They are essentially the gatekeepers for the special ed system. I remember one parent who missed their child's special education meeting steaming into my office yelling, "Who called my kid a retard?" I pointed her in the direction of the psychologist's office as it was her job to determine if a child qualified for a classification and what it would be. At the time mentally retarded was a classification. It was also a word that students often used to disparage and bully each other.

When special education classes were first begun in regular schools, most students were placed in classes where all the kids were classified. It was obvious to the other students that these classes were *special* and as a result, the special kids were easy targets for the local bullies.

When I got my principal job in 1993, there was a push among the innovative special ed teachers to *include* most classified students in regular classes, and provide the services by *pushing* special ed teachers in. This met with a lot of resistance from many general education teachers, as these were the same teachers that worked to push problem kids out into special ed classes so they wouldn't have to deal with them.

In my case I supported the push-in movement and after a few years most of the classified students were receiving help in regular ed classrooms with limited pull out sessions. This brought the number of students in self-contained special ed classes in my school from about 15% down to about 6%. As special ed teachers pushed in to regular classes, they were also able to work with all of the children in the room on occasion, as they helped teachers modify lessons for the special ed kids.

## Poor and Minority Kids

The only students who are considered for special education services are those who fall behind academically. Since poor children are less prepared to perform in school and minority children are more likely to be poor, they are more likely to be candidates for special ed. For this reason, many poor and minority parents see special ed as a stigma and fight the school's efforts to classify their kids.

This is just the opposite with wealthy parents, who push to get their kid classified so they get extra help and extra time on the SATs and other tests. It's just one more way that people who have a lot get more, but it doesn't have to be this way.

## Why Not Just Give Every Kid as Much Time as They Want On Any Test?

As I said in a previous chapter on standardized test cheating, any teacher who calls time on their kids during state tests is doing themselves and their kids a disservice. Who's going to know?

As principal, about a third of my kids were minorities. As luck would have it, one of my three Black teachers taught a 12-1 class that contained zero Black kids. Anytime parents of a Black kid who we felt needed special ed services told me that the program was prejudiced, I just took them to the special ed class with the Black teacher and twelve White students.

Unfortunately, that is not the case in most schools due to the fact that Black kids are more likely to come from poor homes. My sense is that any special ed kid who can spend a lot of time in regular classes is lucky. In order to make it in society, you need to deal with a normal cross section of the population. You are also better off seeing how the higher achieving kids behave and perform.

## The Wealthy and Well Connected Win or How to Beat the System

As I mentioned earlier, parents with means can most likely get their kid classified as they wish. The special ed committee members are not likely to go against parents' wishes and fear being sued.

This happens at both ends of the disabled spectrum. For tests that are high-stakes for kids, parents want a classification to offer kids more time. For parents with kids who have real disabilities, the game changes. What they typically want is the «platinum version» of special ed services. The top shelf service is the one-on-one aide. Pushy parents will even get involved in the selection of the individual aide who follows the student around all day.

Parents with means will often demand that their child be included in regular classes no matter how disabled they are. In addition to extra test time, they also push for individual counseling time every week. Keep in mind that it is the rare school that has extra counseling time available, so when this happens, other kids suffer.

The other problem with poor and minority parents is that they often don't show up to the meetings. Sad to say, it might not matter much if they did, because the test reports from the special ed teacher and the psychologist can sound like Chinese to anyone without a strong background in statistics. Raise your hand if you know what a normal curve equivalent is.

## Meetings, Meetings, and More Meetings

If you do some math on the committee meeting times, it's not a pretty picture. In my school with 530 students, we had a full day of special ed meetings almost every week. Each meeting featured a full-time equivalent of about five employees. For about 30 days of meetings in a 40-week year at an average cost of $10,000 an employee, this creates a yearly cost of about $60,000 which includes hiring substitutes for teachers on the committee. This is very conservative; psychologist and principal salaries are much higher than teacher salaries, and these costs don't include employee benefits. Without the meetings we could easily hire at least another teacher.

The other big expense is the cost of the district special education department. Just about every district has a full-time special ed director with an administrator's certificate. In my district with only 6,000 students we had two. They also have clerks and someone who runs the district meetings caused by situations in which building committees can't sort things out or parents don't agree. For my district this cost is at least $300,000 a year. Districts, however, feel this cost is the price of avoiding law suits.

If schools just were given more teachers with the abilities to help any student who needed it, when they needed it, without committee action, wouldn't we be better off?

## Learning Bad Habits from Each Other

One reason why children with severe disabilities are placed in classes with only special education students is a result of the way some teachers teach. If a class features a one-size-fits-all approach where all students are expected to learn the same thing, at the same time, at the same rate, slow learners will become frustrated and often act out. For many, this is why they get sent off to special ed in the first place. In essence, some teachers cut students off the bottom who can't keep up with the pace the teacher sets.

If classes featured shorter periods of teacher talk, more time for students to work individually or in small groups, and opportunities for peer teaching, students of varying ability would have a better chance of learning together. But in order to keep the kids in a given room somewhat close to each other in terms of ability, kids need to be sorted, which is what the special ed system does at the bottom. (The gifted program does the same at the top, but that's in a later chapter.)

Thanks to the sorting process, schools create what are called self-contained special ed classes. From what I've seen, some are just fine, and some are abusive. There is a wide range. The best classes contain about fifteen slow learners who are well-behaved and who have skilled teachers. Worst case classes are the ones in which eight or so emotionally disturbed kids are in the same room with almost any teacher.

Unfortunately, these jobs have such a high burnout rate that the teachers involved are often relatively inexperienced. In these 8-1 rooms, kids with all sorts of problems get to see endless bad examples from which to learn. This also happens in most schools when both classified and non-classified kids are sent to time-out rooms. In such rooms kids who are having some kind of emotional issue get to see similar behaviors from kids of other classes. They are also usually supervised by less skilled adults than the ones who kicked them out of class in the first place.

## Special Ed and State Standardized Tests

Although the state tests are used to punish teachers and schools and are totally inappropriate for most special ed students, they have to take them anyway. Only the lowest of the low, roughly the bottom 1%, are given alternate testing, which is inconvenient and time-consuming for the teaching staff.

For those unlucky enough to be in the next few percentiles above one percent, the process of taking the tests can feel like punishment. For students with very low reading abilities, the tests are an absolute joke. I've seen kids cry when faced with reading tests they can't read. The scores they do get are always in the bottom level of the four-level system.

When it comes to math, things are a bit better. That's due to the fact that teachers can read the math tests to the students. I guess the geniuses that set up this awful system realized that if you didn't read the math test to the kid you were more or less giving them another *reading* test. Thanks to this accommodation, students do have a shot of getting to level two, and some do. That is still not passing, however, so their teachers stand a good chance of being considered less than effective.

I hesitate to give the testing system too much credit, but it has allowed some self-contained classes to become more academic. Prior to the tests, these classes featured way more fun and games and a stronger focus on life skills. Now they are getting a fairly heavy dose of academic work, and some students seem to like the fact that they are being challenged.

I'm all for pushing these kids academically. Doing so will certainly give them a better chance of decent employment and a happier life. If only we could give them tests that showed what they know instead of tests that just show they don't know much.

## What Happens After Special Ed?

In New York, any child has the legal right to stay in school until age twenty-one. This seldom happens, as schools push kids out to increase their graduation rate. Special ed kids usually end up with something called an IEP diploma as in "Individual Education Plan." Like about half of our current high school graduates, they aren't ready to take college level courses, and probably aren't ready for the high school level courses that two-year colleges give students who fail the placement tests in either English or math.

When we look at data regarding what happens to these students, the picture isn't pretty. Many families and young adults experience the transition to life after graduation not as a launching pad, but as a cliff. Only sixty percent of youths with disabilities are employed for pay outside the home eight years after leaving high school, compared with suxty six percent of all youths. Young adults with disabilities also report earning less money than their non-disabled peers--$10.40 per hour compared with $11.40.

## Is Special Education Racist

In "Is Special Education Racist," Paul L. Morgan and Gorge Farkas claim that special education would appear racist if based on the fact that Black children are 1.4 times as likely to receive special education classifications than other races and ethnicities.

This is faulty logic, however, when you look at the fact that Blacks are much more likely to be poor, and that poor children are much more likely to need the kind of additional attention offered by special education teachers.

According to Morgan and Farkas, however, 65% of Blacks and only 30% of White children live in families below 200% of the poverty line. Blacks are also more likely to have elevated levels of lead in their blood, live in highly disadvantaged neighborhoods, be born premature, and suffer from fetal alcohol syndrome. This means that far more Black children should be candidates for special help.

## What Finland Does: Don't Wait for Gaps to Show.

In Finland, about half of the students who complete compulsory education at the age of sixteen have received some kind of special education service along the way. For any given year the number is one third, with 8% receiving full-time service either in a regular school or a special institution class.

Early intervention is stressed and many children are diagnosed before they enter school. Preschool is free and 98% of the population attends. In my school, the committee of pre-school education removes the classifications they use so the neediest kids show up for kindergarten classification free.

The fraction of Finnish students served by special education staff gradually decreases throughout primary school and goes up a bit during secondary school. This notion of prevention is opposite to most other nations who try to repair students after problems show up. This results in a gradual increase in the number served as students move from grade to grade.

It should be noted that in Finland structural elements that cause failure such as grade retention have also been removed. When someone suggests that we look to Finland for reform ideas, others will quickly respond with statements like Finland is much smaller and more homogeneous than the U.S. What they fail to focus on is that Finland reformed a while ago to the system they have now, which caused significant improvements in their results. It's clear to me that if we were more like Finland, we would get better results.

## What We Should Do

As I said before, old school teaching methods just don't work with students who can't keep up with a teacher's chosen pace. In addition to abolishing committees and classifications, I would just let the teachers figure out who needs extra help and let them have at it. I'm sure they would let me know where the problems were, and I would work with them to smooth things out.

I would retain some of the individual testing when the teachers thought it would help, and I'd make the results available to teachers and parents. I would be sure to let parents know when their children are getting additional help from *consultant* teachers and for what reason.

Instead of treating all students the same, you would ideally treat each individual child the way they need to be treated. Finally, I would seek to eliminate the word special ed from the school culture's lexicon.

As for the current crop of state tests, it would be fine with me if every kid opted out. I'm encouraged by the large increase of parents opting kids out in New York this year (2016); many schools had more than half of their kids do so. We need to get some laws changed to do what I suggest, but we also need to change some laws to end the test and punish madness we are now experiencing.

My goal here is to get educators, parents, and policy makers thinking about what could be a better system for children in need. What we have now has some positive aspects, but there is lots of room for improvement.

In the meantime, we also need administrators with backbones, who are more concerned about what is best for students and less concerned about following rules that waste precious funds and prevent teachers from doing their best. For more on this subject be sure to check out Miriam Kurtzig Freedman's fine book *Special Education 2.0: Breaking Taboos to Build a NEW Education Law*. You can start with my summary here: http://bit.ly/2pqZVa2 .

# References
Center for Public Education, "How many students with disabilities are in our school(s)?" http://bit.ly/1UlR83Z

Kurtzig Freedman, Miriam (2017). *Special Education 2.0: Breaking Taboos to Build a NEW Education Law*, Kurtzig Freedman: New York, NY.

Laws and Guidance: Special Education & Rehabilitation Services, US Department of Education. Twenty-Five Years of Progress in Educating Children with Disabilities Through IDEA, downloaded June 15,2017, http://bit.ly/2s5fSXv.

Morgan, Paul L and Farkas, Gorge, Is Special Education Racist?, New York Times, June 24, 2015, P. A21.

Samuels, Christina. Students Face Uncertain Paths After Special Education, downloaded June 15, 2017 http://bit.ly/1RPfmkS.

# CHAPTER 9

# Shouldn't All Students Be Able to Participate in Gifted Programs?

"If gifted classes are so good, why can't all students take part?"
-Dr. Doug Green

MOST OF THIS chapter was published as a post in EdWeek Teacher Online in 2015. It drew far more comments than any other article I have ever written and most of the comments were negative. Some were from parents who claimed to have profoundly gifted children who they thought deserved special lessons. Some were from gifted teachers who apparently weren't excited about dealing with "non-gifted" students. In spite of the criticism, I'm sticking to my guns in the hope that I can persuade some of my critics.

## Setting Up the Gifted Program

Programs for so-called gifted students exist in most school districts in the United States today, and they vary widely in size and scope. Some districts have gifted teachers who travel from school to school, while others have their own full-time gifted teachers in each school.

To set up such a program, a school needs to do two things. They need to come up with a program for the gifted teacher to roll out, and they need a system for selecting the gifted students. No matter how you do this, it involves drawing an arbitrary line somewhere along the continuum of scores or ratings earned by all students.

## Culling the Gifted

Most schools at least look at standardized test scores of some sort to identify gifted students. Such tests are usually designed to sort students along a low to high achievement or intelligence spectrum. At any point, the difference between one student and the next one, up or down in terms of scores, is negligible at best.

A score on such a test usually locates a child within a range of scores with a certain degree of certainty. This means that a child with a slightly higher score than a classmate can be less accomplished than the lower scoring child. Any school that simply draws a line on a continuum of test scores is certainly leaving out some students who are more gifted than some of the chosen.

Schools that also use teacher recommendations most likely do a better job of selecting students who are more capable. I hesitate to use the term gifted as it implies an artificial dichotomy. Unfortunately, schools that use teacher recommendations as the initial filter tend to identify fewer Black students even when they have the same abilities and backgrounds.

Certainly some students are more advanced in terms of reading, math, problem solving, and creative thinking than others, but I've never been in favor of drawing lines that separate students into gifted and non-gifted categories. This only serves to anoint some as gifted and everyone else as second rate. In a previous chapter I also said that I didn't think that we should tell some students that they were "special ed" either.

What complicates the selection process further in many schools are parents who lobby for their children to be placed in the gifted program. What chance does a principal have when a parent with a friend on the Board of Education wants their kid in the program when they didn't make the cut?

## Pull-Out Program Characteristics

In many cases, the gifted teacher takes the identified students out of their classes to a room where they engage in the program's activities. These activities tend to be interesting, engaging, and usually hands on. They are much more likely to involve science activities than what goes on in the regular classroom. Elementary teachers as a group don't tend to be strong in either math or science so this is a good place to go for the gifted teacher.

Students left in the class who didn't make the cut can't move on to new material that their gifted chums would miss, so they are destined to review material and skills that they may or may not be so good at. A great way to turn kids off to school is to avoid doing anything new. This process can lessen the motivation of non-gifted students and their non-gifted classroom teacher.

## What Should We Do?

If I had control of this type of program, I would tell the gifted teacher to provide the program to all students. The initial benefit would be to not waste time and effort on sorting kids in the first place. You also stop labeling students and no longer have unhappy parents in your face. Every student could tell their parents about how they are in the gifted program.

This is exactly what happened in the school where I was principal. We called the program The Challenge Program and the teacher who delivered it was The Challenge Teacher. Once a week each class got a special lesson, which the students eagerly awaited.

Most gifted lessons I've seen have been open-ended, interesting, and engaging. They deal with new material, which means that background knowledge is less of an issue. Since all students participate, the classroom teachers are also involved and get a dose of professional development in the process.

The regular teacher can trot out the same gifted lessons next year and the gifted teacher works on new lessons for next year. Gifted classes can be bigger because the classroom teacher or teachers stay there to assist the gifted teacher. If the class features a consulting special education teacher, so much the better.

Thanks to the hands-on nature of many gifted lessons, special ed students should be able to participate. Their disabilities usually involve things like reading rather than doing things with their hands. I've seen classes where one or more special ed kids did better manipulating real objects than the more academically accomplished students.

## What to do with the Seriously Gifted

As for the so-called profoundly gifted students, who are few in number, the gifted teacher, along with building leadership, should look for some individual activities, projects, and opportunities that can specifically challenge students. This is what I did as a teacher and principal. In one case I let a student take AP chemistry as an independent study course under my supervision. As the central office computer director I hired the top students as programmers. They usually solved the problems that I couldn't figure out.

I also facilitated rides to neighboring colleges so students could take college courses for credit as they mopped up the requirements for high school graduation during the rest of the day. One student I had that did this took so much math in high school that the first math course he took as a freshman at Harvard was abstract algebra.

On occasion I had to take on the district bureaucracy to let students get ahead. One student asked why he couldn't take the next math course in summer school. At the time the school's policy said that summer school was only for students retaking courses they failed. After several attempts, I finally wore the principal down. I said that I would be responsible for teaching the student the third high school math course during the summer prior to his sophomore year. He said ok, but that the kid had to get an 85 on the state final.

All I did was give the student a copy of the textbook and some old state exams and told him the date of the state final. I did nothing else as I knew this student had become a self-directed learner at an early age. With no help from me other than cutting some red tape, the student sailed though the course. Compared to other disciplines, math has relatively few concepts to master. For this reason, it is one area were the ultra smart can move much faster than their classmates.

## A Final Word or Two

If you skim kids off the top of the distribution for special lessons, you almost doom the rest of the students to fewer opportunities which will inspire excitement about school and learning. To me this is unethical and wrong. Thanks to many gifted programs the rich get richer. That's not what schools should be doing by design.

If we can build a system that allows *all* students to move at their own pace, there would be little need for "gifted" programs. I would keep the current crop of gifted teachers, however, as they can be a rich source of professional development for classroom teachers and assist in putting programs together for the students who are ready for additional challenges. See my chapter on flipping your class for some details on how this can be accomplished.

## References

Green, Douglas W. Shouldn't All Students Be Able to Participate in Gifted Programs? *Education Week Online*, *09/29/2015* http://bit.ly/1KNQvb6

Grissom, Jason A. Why Do Fewer Black Students Get Identified as Gifted? *The Edvocate Online*, February 3, 2016, http://bit.ly/2t1xUXz.

CHAPTER **10**

# Education Drugs:
# Learning on Steroids

"If education is a sport, it's time to clean it up in terms of drug use." -Dr. Doug Green

I GREW UP in a small town in western New York where the drugs available to high school students were alcohol and nicotine. My high school in the 60s didn't even feature the caffeine-laced Mountain Dew let alone Red Bull and other high energy drinks.

While there may have been other drugs floating around town, none were very mainstream or available. When I started college in 1965 things weren't much different. By the time the late '60s rolled around, marijuana had hit big time. My fraternity parties went from seven kegs of beer a night to two kegs with a big room upstairs where you could almost get high without actually smoking anything.

Another drug innovation of the time were diet pills. I went to Clarkson University in rural Potsdam, New York, which was 95% male and 95% science, business, or engineering majors. Across town was Potsdam State. It was mostly women and the most popular major was education. It was the rare fraternity date that didn't come from "State."

47

While the boys at Clarkson had to get by with alcohol, weed, and nicotine, our girlfriends became a source for uppers in the guise of "diet pills." I'm not sure of the exact name of the drug in question, but it was certainly a member of the amphetamine club. At the time I had a girlfriend who could ill afford to lose any weight, but that didn't stop her from scoring diet pills from the college infirmary.

While I suspected that the girls were popping pills for fun and for study reasons, they were happy to share them with their boyfriends. Word got out around my fraternity that we should use these babies on nights when we had to study for a big test. This is exactly what I did. Thanks to my girlfriend's study drugs, I'm sure that I scored much higher grades on a number of finals during my junior and senior years. Fortunately, my brothers and I never got into these for recreational use. That was no doubt a good thing.

## The New Study Drugs

Fast forward to today where we find "study drugs" being passed out in elementary school. I'm glad that ADHD hadn't been invented when I was a kid. Now that it has, we have kids taking drugs so they can "focus" in class. For the most part, this means that they are more likely to be able to sit still and be compliant, which is what adults prefer.

Once a child demonstrates behavior that is inconvenient for the teachers, some teachers, with the help of administration, push parents to take the kid to a doctor and ask for ADHD drugs. Unfortunately, many doctors are only too happy to comply.

Rather than adapt to students who have a hard time sitting still, many teachers push the young version of study drugs. It's important to note that some teachers see this drug push as bad for students. They adapt by allowing restless students to stand while they are working or letting them sit on exercise balls. They also make sure that teacher talk is limited to ten minutes or less at a time and make direct instruction available online.

On the parental side, we see poor parents being bullied into getting drugs for their kids. Unfortunately, these are the kind of parents who are less likely to make sure that their kids take their drugs on a regular basis. They are most likely to forget to refill the prescription and see that the school nurse gets the lunch time doses every day. There is also the temptation to take these drugs for recreational purposes or sell them on the street.

This type of parental neglect results in kids going on and off drugs and teachers getting upset as students with improved focus regress. I saw a great deal of this as principal and was constantly being badgered by teachers to get parents to hold up their end of the deal. This adds stress to families who can ill afford it and can't be good for kids.

## The Money Issue

According to WIRED Magazine, ADHD drugs are a $13 billion industry in the United States, and ADHD is now the second most-common childhood diagnosis. But even though the long term effects of these amphetamines on the childhood brain are unknown, the numbers will probably continue to rise.

The American Psychiatric Association, which has recently expanded the criteria for ADHD diagnosis, receives 20 to 30 percent of its funding from pharmaceutical companies. The main organization for the support of ADHD children and adults, Children and Adults with Attention-Deficit/Hyperactivity Disorder (CHADD), receives over $1 million a year from companies that manufacture ADHD medication. CHADD also publishes a variety of printed materials to keep members and professionals current on research advances, medications and treatments affecting individuals with ADHD. I should note that it doesn't seem like CHADD overtly pushes or discourages medication. See their website for more at http://chadd.org.

## The Fairness Issue

Then there is the matter of fairness where these drugs are concerned. When it comes to high stakes tests, these drugs do seem to work in the short term. It certainly wasn't fair that I had access to study drugs in college when many of my classmates didn't.

Likewise, it isn't fair that some kids get to take test drugs while others don't. In some cases parents and their doctors are responsible. In other cases, kids with money can obtain them illegally, perhaps in some cases from the parents of poor kids with ADHD diagnoses.

If you haven't guessed it by now, this is a very strong analogy to the situation in sports where some players take performance-enhancing drugs, while others don't. In baseball, for instance, we have already seen how players with a known record of taking PEDs have been denied Hall of Fame status. The situation involving Lance Armstrong also comes to mind.

Is there any doubt that at least some students made it to elite colleges thanks to their access to study drugs? Should they have an asterisk next to their names like Barry Bonds, Alex Rodriguez, and other steroid users?

In addition to the fairness factor, I have no doubt that some kids who take ADHD drugs will suffer from side effects. If education is a sport, it's time to clean it up in terms of drug use. Stop giving drugs to kids who can't sit still. Teachers need to create classrooms where kids can stand and move about so that they don't stick out as kids who can't sit still.

## ADHD Can Lead to Success

Kids with ADHD can have attributes that allow them to succeed after school, and there are many successful adults who can testify to this. If you as a parent don't have access to enlightened schools and your kid's teacher is pushing drugs, fight back. If you can, look for charter, private, or other public schools who understand how to deal with antsy kids. Also consider home schooling where kids don't have to sit still for most of the day.

At the same time, teachers and school leaders need to build in more opportunities for all kids to move during the day. In the school where I used to be a principal, even kindergarteners are expected to focus on reading instruction for ninety continuous minutes every day.

For many kids, this looks like a recipe for getting more kids to hate school sooner.

This academic push is happening because the adults in the system think that the more academic work they give students of any age, the better they will do on state tests, which is primarily in the best interests of the adults. The use of drugs and long periods of strictly academic work are good for adults, but in my opinion, bad for kids. Recent news reports indicated that ADHD drugs can lead to the use of more powerful versions such as methamphetamine. It's time to stop this madness.

# References
Sackstein, Starr. Tableau Installations and Kinesthetic Literature: Movement can't be underrated in the classroom, EdWeek Teacher Online, February 9, 2015, http:///2s95E8b.

WIRED Staff. ADHD Drugs Make Big Money But We Still Don't Know the Risks. WIREDD Online, Swcwmber 9, 2015, http://bit. ly/2rGOBa4.

# CHAPTER 11

# Kindergarten is the New First Grade

"In Finland the real academic effort doesn't kick in until kids turn seven, and they kick our butts on international tests." -Dr. Doug Green

WHEN I STARTED my principal's job in 1993, my kindergarten classes were almost identical to today's pre-school classes. Somewhere along the way kindergarten classes turned into programs that are very much like the first grade classes of the 1990s and earlier.

In 1993, the typical kindergarten class featured stations around the room where students could essentially play with educational toys such as wooden blocks, Legos, and other toys where students started with a pile of pieces and had to build something without instructions or a model to duplicate. There were art stations that featured crayons and large easels with messy liquid paint and brushes and a sand box. At these stations, students started with a blank canvas and were challenged to draw or make something of their choice. Other art stations featured scissors, colored paper, and glue.

The classroom had a library of picture books that contained few, if any words. At times all students would gather on the floor while the teacher read a book or carried out some other kind of direct instruction. The amount of time sitting still and listening was a small fraction of the total time, and students spent a good deal of time moving and socializing. Sometimes the movement was organized by the teacher in the form of dance or exercise, but much of it was independent.

Once in the morning and once in the afternoon, the class was taken to the playground where they were usually in constant motion for about half an hour. Mid-morning was snack time when students ate what they brought and talked freely to other students. Since 90% of my students were poor, we made sure that we had nutritious snacks for students who brought none.

After lunch, which featured another trip to the playground, students had nap time, which usually lasted about fifteen minutes. This was followed by more action similar to what took place in the morning. As for academics, they were limited to letter, number, and short sight word recognition along with colors and shapes. There was an emphasis on manners and other appropriate social and emotional behavior, along with following the teacher's instructions.

## No More Free-Range Children

By the 1990s, the day of the free-range student had mostly ended, at least in my small city of Binghamton, New York. I know this because I often made home visits after school. As I drove about my neighborhoods, it was rare to see one or more children outside without an adult. During my childhood in the 1950s, when kids got home from school they were usually told to play outside without constraints and to be home in time for dinner.

In my case I spent a lot of time playing in a local dump and a swamp at the end of the street. I often was armed with metal-tipped arrows for my bow and a BB gun. My range was as far as I could go on my bike and still get home for dinner. By the time I was in fifth grade, this range was up to three miles in any direction. I also played in the railroad yard and sometimes hopped a short ride.

Any parent today who allowed this kind of behavior would likely have their kids taken away from them. Kids in my neighborhood organized games of all sorts without the help of any adults and often made up our own games. We played games in the street and simply got out of the way when cars came along. Even at my elementary school the softball games during lunch time and the playground in general lacked any adult supervision. In spite of this I don't remember ever seeing a fight.

## The Kindergarten of 2017

When I retired in 2006, my district was just starting a program called *Reading First*. The primary hallmark of this program was a 90-minute reading block every morning for *every grade*. That's right, kindergarten students were expected to engage in reading lessons for 90 continuous minutes. Jeez! While this might work for wealthy kids who have lots of experience with language and a year or two of preschool, all it does for poor kids is make them dislike school sooner. Imagine spending 90 minutes doing something you essentially can't do, or at least can't do very well.

Since I retired, I've done a lot of consulting and visited a lot of schools. I've also observed many classes at all grade levels. What I have seen in today's kindergartens features much less movement about the room. Kids spend most of their time sitting and building blocks are nowhere to be seen.

There are still stations around the room, but they all feature some kind of academic work. Groups of students might be reading books, writing stories, and doing math computations using computer tablets. They still use crayons and markers to draw pictures but now they have to write stories below the pictures. Don't plan on finding big easels and messy wet paint or a sandbox either.

Naps and trips to the playground with the exception of lunchtime recess are gone, and some schools have cut back on recess and replaced it with more academic time. You can still find teachers reading books while students gather on the floor. You should also see teachers showing short videos on the classroom whiteboard, but they will probably reinforce the never-ending academic grind.

Kindergarten students are still likely to be more excited than older students, but there is a lot less fun. If you talk to veteran teachers, they are likely to tell you that kindergarten is indeed what first grade was ten or more years ago.

We should look to Finland, a country that usually finishes among the top countries on international tests. While our kids are grinding away, they are mostly playing. According to Timothy Walker, writing for *The Atlantic*, Finland's kindergartners spend a sizable chunk of each day playing, not filling out worksheets. In Finland the real academics kick in when kids turn seven.

## Is This Good for Kids?

Is never-ending academics good for kids? I certainly can't say for certain, but I don't think so, and I am concerned. So far efforts to cram more academic time into earlier grades hasn't resulted in higher NEAP test scores. Less movement might be exacerbating our national obesity/diabetes epidemic. Less emphasis on music could be an issue as music ability is often associated with higher cognitive ability. Less emphasis on art could have implications for spatial intelligence down the road. Less time socializing in unstructured ways is yet another concern. If you are looking for a long list of academic references on this topic that support my concerns, see Bassok, Latham, and Rorem's *Is Kindergarten the New First Grade*.

## References

Bassok, D., Latham, S. & Rorem, A. (2016). Is Kindergarten the New First Grade. AERA Open, 1(4), 1-31, DOI: 10.1177/2332858415616358, http://bit.ly/2qrt0Fy.

Walker, Timothy. The Joyful, Illiterate Kindergartners of Finland, October 1, 2015, *The Atlantic*, http://theatln.tc/2pW04BS.

# CHAPTER 12

# Math Class: The Champ at Slowing Down the Fast Learners

"The only way to close achievement gaps is to slow down the fast learners." -Dr. Doug Green

COMPARED TO OTHER disciplines, mathematics has a much smaller number of concepts to learn. As a result, the students with high math ability are often needlessly held back. They also run the risk of boredom and/or acting out during math classes.

At the other end, students with poor math skills get dragged on to new concepts before they master current lessons. Since much of math is hierarchical in nature, not mastering early lessons can make later lessons impossible to comprehend. This is less of an issue in other content areas. While other lessons often rely on background knowledge from previous lessons, students who don't master previous lessons can still appreciate new material to some degree.

The one-size-fits-all single pace approach that many teachers still use is, therefore, more of a problem in math class than elsewhere. By the time middle school rolls around, most schools sort students into advanced and regular math classes. This is done so that the top students can take some variation of algebra in eighth grade for which they receive high school credit. To do this, teachers cram two years of math into the curriculum for the advanced kids. Why it only happens during this one year makes *no sense!*

Taking a year of high school math in eighth grade allows students who desire it to take four more years of math during their high school career for a total of five credits. The final credit is usually some variation of calculus that may include an Advanced Placement class, at the end of which is the national AP exam in May, which might allow some students to start their college careers with calculus II or III.

## Catching the Calculus Train

Students who take calculus in high school are well positioned to major in engineering or physical science in college. Students who miss the eighth grade algebra train most likely won't be able to take calculus their senior year, and will be at a huge disadvantage if they want to pursue engineering or physical science.

This so-called train actually leaves the station for most students at the beginning of seventh grade. In order to take what amounts to math 9 in eighth grade, teachers have to cram math 7 and math 8 into the seventh grade year. This requires schools to identify candidates for the advanced math program near the end of sixth grade.

In my case, my school gave some standardized tests to sixth graders. As fate would have it, I was absent for these tests. Rather than ask the teacher if I was advanced math material, I was dumped into the seventh grade section that was one notch above the class that contained students with major cognitive issues.

This meant that I couldn't take calculus my senior year, but that didn't stop me from majoring in chemistry. During my calculus I class in my freshman college year, the teacher asked the class who had calculus in high school. As I looked around I noticed that I was one of only two students who didn't raise his hand. Ouch!

I struggled, of course, but nonetheless managed to graduate. My lack of calculus in high school, however, affected not only my math grades but grades in physics and physical chemistry. This meant that my career options did not include a PhD in chemistry. I decided to pick up a masters in education and go into teaching. I guess I can't complain as I have enjoyed a great deal of success as an educator and wouldn't change my decision to teach if I could.

As I stated earlier, the main point here is if the top students can do two years of math in seventh grade, why can't they do more than one year of math in every other grade including earlier grades? The answer, of course, is that they can. It's just that most schools don't make it possible. (See the story of my efforts to help math students advance in my gifted chapter.)

## Top Math Students Outshine Their Teachers

Due to the smallish number of concepts in math, it isn't unusual for the top students to go beyond their teachers while still in high school. This also happens in music but almost nowhere else, as it takes time to develop the knowledge base necessary for other subjects like science and history.

While I was computer director, I took part in a knowledge competition involving the high school faculty. This involved a timed test taken as a group. A student team also competed. While the faculty beat the students badly on non-math topics, the students routinely clobbered the faculty on the math questions. This was in spite of the fact that the faculty team included several math teachers.

## Top Math Students Seldom Go Into Teaching

Students who are good at math have a lot of options. As a result, few of them go into teaching and almost none become elementary or middle school teachers. Since the U.S. educates more teachers than it needs in some areas like elementary education, education is often seen as an easy major on most campuses. This is just the opposite in Finland where you need to be in the top 10% to be accepted into a teacher preparation program and they only prepare as many teachers as they need.

People who major in elementary education tend to have even lower math skills and the teacher prep programs do little to address this. Most require only a single math course or two, and they tend to be pretty simple. If you are wondering why the Common Core math results seem to be stuck at low levels, keep in mind that a few days of staff development will not turn teachers with poor or average math skills and bad attitudes into math whizzes.

The other big problem in the math area shows up when students head off to college. This shows up to the greatest degree at the community college level. Community colleges tend to be open enrollment, so anyone who wants to go and finds the money can enroll. Since these colleges know that their incoming students aren't all of the blue chip variety, they make them take placement tests in language arts and math.

When I asked the math chair at my local community college how students do on the placement test, he told me that two thirds don't pass. This means that they have to take what amounts to high school math in college for which they have to pay though they don't receive college credit. Many of these same students also flunk the language arts test. What this means is that these students have very little chance of picking up a two-year degree in two years. Studies I have seen indicate that my local college is typical of other two-year schools in the U.S. in this regard. (See the next chapter for more detail on this topic.).

## Flip It, Flip It Good

During the last decade, there has been an increased interest in flipping classes. (See my chapter on flipping near the end of this book.) This is where students watch direct instructional videos at home or in school. This frees the teacher up to help students individually or in small groups during class time.

An extension of this plan is called flipped-mastery. This where students take unit tests when they think they are ready. If they don't exhibit mastery, they work with the teacher to learn what they missed and then retake the unit test until they master it. This can allow some students to finish courses in less than a year while others can just keep on going during the summer or the next school year to finish.

This plan replaces the concept of "You Failed; Go Back to Square One" with the concept of "You Haven't Finished Yet so Keep on Plugging Away." Of all the subjects, I think that math lends itself to this type of instruction very well. Also check my summary of *Flip Your Class: Reach Every Student in Every Classroom Every Day* by Jonathan Bergmann and Arron Sams for more information on flipping at http://bit.ly/1atBiOe. Then purchase this fine book for your school's professional development library.

## What to Do?

No matter how you do it, do what you can to make math more self-paced for all students. It may not be the most convenient thing for adults, but I firmly believe it's the best for *all* students. It rewards hard work and takes failure out of the game. If done right, it will also result in a greater difference in achievement for fast and slow learners alike as all learners will most likely learn more.

There is also no excuse for not giving high school students the placement tests as juniors so they can get remediation for free while they are still in high school. I also suggest that school leaders grow a backbone and stop booting unprepared students out just to polish their graduation rates.

This stat is totally meaningless to individual students, and in case you haven't heard, schools are supposed to be in business for the sake of the students, not the adults and the arbitrary demands of the corporate/political class.

## References

National Center for Education Statistics. *First-Year Undergraduate Remedial Course taking: 1999-2000, 2003-04, 2007-08*, January, 2013, http://1.usa.gov/1gvjWqZ.

Reyna, Ryan. *Common College Completions Metrics*, NGA Center for Best Practices Education Division, June 2010, http://bit.ly/1GfxlZg.

CHAPTER **13**

# Not Ready for College?
# Flunk Gym.

"Graduating students who aren't ready to take college English
or math courses is malpractice in my book." -Dr. Doug Green

THANKS TO PRESSURE from the federal government, high schools
are pressed to increase their four-year graduation rates. Unfortunately,
this is easy to do by simply making it easier to graduate, and many
high schools seem to have done so. This is similar in nature to schools
that cheat on the federally mandated tests.

The unintended consequence of graduating students who aren't
ready for college is the expansion of remedial courses by colleges.
While colleges still charge tuition for these courses, they are not
credit bearing. They are also big money makers, as the classes tend
to be large and at some schools two thirds of incoming students have
to take at least one. This situation is shameful and both high schools
and colleges should be held responsible for caring about their institution's bottom lines and graduation rates more than their customers,
the students.

Unless a student has "high grades," students have to take placement tests in English and math. They are given by almost all two-year

schools and some public four-year schools during the spring semester of a student's senior year. Few high schools offer preparation courses for these exams other than the English and math courses the students take along the way.

As stated in the last chapter, for math this is really problematic as most students don't take math during their senior year since it isn't required. Some may even stop taking math sooner. This means that their preparation for the test involves not studying the subject for a year or more prior to test day. Many schools also charge for these tests to cover the costs they bear from the people who make the tests.

## So What Should High Schools And Colleges Do To Deal With This Injustice?

First they should work together to help students pass the placement tests before they start paying tuition. It shouldn't be too difficult to improve their current state of practice, but it does require a leadership vision that says the status quo is unacceptable, and for my money, immoral and/or unethical.

Step one would be to administer the placement tests at the end of their junior year to let every student know if they are ready or not. Students who aren't ready in either or both subjects can then use their entire senior year and the prior summer to get ready.

Step two would suggest that high schools design senior electives aimed at preparing students for the tests. For some students, they will probably be able to pass the test mid-year. This would allow for some more interesting electives during the second semester.

Students that still don't pass mid-year can redouble their efforts. But no matter how hard they try, some will still not be ready at the end of their senior year. Ideally, students who aren't ready shouldn't graduate but if they must, some kind of post-graduate program for these students should be available in the fifth year for free. As this would probably be a part-time affair, these same students should be able to take a few college courses in other subjects as non-matriculated students at the local two-year school to get some experience with college.

## Know When to Flunk Gym

For students who do not attend enlightened high schools that offer programs similar to the one suggested, they can take matters into their own hands. I'm sure colleges would be happy to give placement tests to juniors for a fee, so if the high school doesn't make this happen, students can do it themselves. Test results should help to design a senior year course plan. If at the end of the senior year the student still isn't ready, the goal should be to return to high school the following year for courses that will prepare students properly.

If students attend a high school that is determined to graduate them anyway, and won't allow them to return as post graduates, students may have to resort to doing what it takes to not graduate on their own.

At my local high school this would simply involve failing the last semester of physical education. (Apologies to PE teachers for the title, but these classes do usually take place in the gym.) Flunking gym was easy at my school since all you had to do to fail was not show up.

Let's hope that schools will cooperate with students needing more time with high school level courses so they won't have to resort to this type of subterfuge. And if your high school is still pushing kids out to pay college tuition for high school courses, for god's sake do something about it. It isn't that complicated.

## References

Brody, Leslie, Just 37% of U.S. High School Seniors Prepared for College Math and Reading, Test Shows, *The Wall Street Journal*, 5/2/2016, http://on.wsj.com/2qL2zL6.

College Board Access Staff. What Are College Placement Tests? Big Future by the College Board, May 4, 2016, http://bit.ly/1ZcRAlq.

Kamenetz, Anya, Most High School Seniors Aren't College Or Career Ready, Says 'Nation's Report Card', NPR Ed Online, 5/2/2016, http://n.pr/1SFO0Qw.

# CHAPTER 14

# Coding for Everyone, Are You Serious, Mr. President?

"I'm not even sure why everyone has to take algebra, let alone computer programming." -Dr. Doug Green

WHILE HE WAS still in office, President Obama joined the mayors of New York and Chicago and called for federal legislation that would *require* computer programming to be part of the curriculum for all students. Here I consider a contrary view and what I think we should consider instead.

In 1976 I invented and taught a programming course for high school students. At the time we had one computer and thirty-one students who signed up for a brand new one semester course. While I did my best, I doubt the course was of high quality.

As time went on, I'm sure I improved and I eventually moved on to direct the entire computer operation in a larger district (Binghamton, New York). There I had a teacher with a degree in computer science who had experience and expertise. Students could take two years of computer science and the classes were packed. This was 1985. As time went on, demand decreased and when the teacher retired, the courses were dropped altogether.

Today, only 25 percent of high schools offer computer science and less than five percent offer the AP computer science course. There is also an economic and racial gap since the courses are taught less often in schools that serve poor and minority students. By pushing coding for all, whatever incremental success we have will largely benefit the elites.

## Why It Won't Happen

If every student had to take a programming course, every school would have to recruit and hire multiple new teachers. Why would anyone with a degree in computer science go into teaching at a time when current reforms have made teaching less attractive even to students who have degrees that are less in demand?

According to the New York Times, computer science students can expect an average starting salary of $61,300, while the average starting teacher salary is $34,900. To make things worse, the computer science major would need at least a year in graduate school to become certified, barring changes in each state's teacher certification laws. I think it's fair to say that the small trickle of computer science majors entering the teaching field may not even be enough to maintain today's meager offerings.

I'm sure people pushing coding for all believe that we can take some existing teachers and turn them into computer science teachers with a few professional development days. Sorry folks, you can't cram a four-year major into the kind of workshops for which schools are noted. For the same reason, such workshops haven't even been effective in turning non-math majors into effective math teachers.

If you remember the push to teach Logo in the 1980s and 1990s, it involved innovative teachers making students move a virtual turtle around the screen. From what I saw, most teachers rejected the idea and as a result it never caught on. While it was "coding," it never approached the kind of coding one would need to do to create useful software. A lot of what passes for coding today falls into the category which I call "coding lite."

## Why It Probably Shouldn't Happen

Fortunately, we don't have to worry about any serious effort to teach real computer science to every child and in my view, this is a good thing. I know a number of people who create professional level software, and they are a special breed in terms of ability and work ethic.

Expecting all students to create anything worthwhile is unrealistic. Just having to learn the ins and outs of a real programming language would bore and frustrate most students. In short, it isn't easy and it isn't fun, at least at first. Anyone who has learned a programming language knows that it starts with rote learning and no real-world connection. While the fast learners will be solving problems in a creative way, I doubt that most students will get to this point.

In addition to exposing many students to lessons that they will find frustrating and boring, you will also have to stop exposing them to something else. Students who already suffer from an overemphasis on the reading and math content found on state tests at the expense of subjects like social studies, science, the arts and recess, don't need this. If only the corporate/political class would stop forcing what they see as good ideas on schools. They have done enough damage already.

## What Should Happen Instead

We want to engage students in critical thinking and open-ended problem solving as we put them in situations where they can express their creativity as they deal with interesting real-world content. There are ways we can do this and still allow them to rub up against concepts associated with computer programming such as conditional reasoning and iteration.

Many schools have opened Maker Spaces where students can build things using their own designs. A reader of my blog recently sent information about a device called X-Carve that lets you carve anything you can design, using the software that comes with it. Some schools have clubs that design and build robots and fly drones. You need to use elements of programming here, but you don't need to learn intense nerdy languages like C++, Javascript, or python.

In 1996 as an elementary principal, I taught myself HTML so I could program my school's first web page. Since then, a number of 4th generation programming languages have come along that let you create web pages without having to know the underlying language.

There are also tools for creating blogs that do not require knowing a standard programming language. Many other applications that let you create things like spreadsheets and presentations have some programming attributes. More access to real computer science courses is also available online as long as teachers unions cooperate.

In short, there are lots of ways that all students can learn how to control computers that have immediate real-world impact and can involve student interest, passion, problem solving and creativity. There are also many innovative teachers supporting these tools whom others need to try to follow. Leadership is key, but it should come from people with educational expertise and not politicians and corporate big wigs.

## References

Cohen, Patricia. A Rising Call to Promote STEM Education and Cut Liberal Arts Funding, *New York Times* February 22, 2016, p. B1 http://nyti.ms/21jfJMD.

Inventables. X-Carve: Make Real Stuff With 3D Carving. It comes with the design software. This looks like a great addition to the maker space in your school. http://bit.ly/1QzVVJF

McClure, Laura. 5 places where any kid can learn how to code. If your kids are going to learn how to code they will probably have to do it online. *TED-Ed Lessons,* February 17, 2016 http://bit.ly/1Tprdbo.

Strauss, Valerie. All students should learn to code. Right? Not so fast. Proponents of coding for all should read this. Anyone remember Logo? *Washington Post,* January 30, 2016 http://wapo.st/1nYC68v.

Wilensky, Uri. Why schools need to introduce computing in all subjects, *The Edvocate,* February 10, 2016 http://bit.ly/1QbCV8v.

CHAPTER **15**

# SATs For All? One More Bad Idea From The Political Elite.

"Thanks to the vision of a politician, students in New York City now have one more required standardized test that is sure to frustrate many." -Dr. Doug Green

ON MARCH 2, 2016, juniors at 92 New York City high schools opened their test booklets and took the new SAT during regular school hours. Next year this program will expand to all city high schools thanks to Mayor Bill de Blasio's conviction that it will serve to make college more accessible for more city students.

Just how low performing students who otherwise would not take this test benefit is beyond me. Almost all of these additional students are candidates for open-door two-year schools that don't require the test or even a high school diploma. These are not students who are candidates for the decreasing number of competitive schools that still require the SAT or its competitor, the ACT.

Thanks to the vision of a politician, students in New York City now have one more required standardized test that is sure to frustrate many poor and minority students and make them feel even more like failures. I know you can't technically fail an SAT, but students will know if they are doing well or not.

This test will also take time away from something else in schools which have already been spending too much time prepping and taking ELA and math tests at the expense of things like social studies, science, the arts, physical education, and recess.

## Another Chance to Fail

How does giving a test to poor kids help when the results of the SAT are already strongly correlated with income by zip code? If low SAT scores have kept successful students out of college as David O'Hara, the principal of Leaders High School in Gravesend, Brooklyn claims, how does simply giving the test to all make any difference? Mr. O'Hara also admits that there is no funding for a Saturday class for the additional students who will be taking the test. In essence, New York City is giving many students a test for which they are not prepared. If this isn't malpractice, I don't know what else to call it.

Keep in mind that this is happening in light of recent findings that one's GPA trumps the SAT in predicting college success, and that every year more colleges become test optional. By taking more time away from class activities that lead toward grades and one's GPA, it seems that diverting time to take the SAT could only have a negative impact on student access to college and success once they arrive.

## Oh Boy, A Brand New SAT

To make matters worse, this is the first year for the "new SAT." A recent New York Times article reveals that the new test features longer and more difficult reading passages on the reading part, and more reading on the math part, making it more of a reading test. The article claims that the average readability on the new test is at least a grade level higher.

This is bad news for English Language Learners and other students with disabilities who find reading challenging as it is. It also means that the test is totally inappropriate for even more students. Giving the SAT to students in the bottom percentiles of student achievement seems like abuse to me.

While I'm all for making the test available for free to poor students, I see no reason for taxpayers to foot the bill for wealthier kids. This is just one more way the rich get richer as these are the same students whose parents can also afford to pay for SAT prep classes beyond the school day. It's ironic that a mayor who claims to be a champion of the poor has put in place a program that gives the haves another free step up the ladder of success.

SATs for all is another reflection of how education continues to suffer from reforms mandated by politicians from both sides of the political spectrum with encouragement from corporate elites. Schools are also run by school boards composed of elected volunteers who for the most part also lack real educational expertise. I respect the time and devotion that school board members give, but let me know if you are aware of any business where the people at the top lack strong expertise in the business they run.

Lack of expertise at the top is one reason why schools and businesses differ. The second factor that separates schools from businesses is that schools, or at least public schools, have no control over their raw materials. Expecting schools to be run like a business is, in a word, *insane!* That doesn't mean that educators can't learn from some of what business does. I know I have. It does mean that business people and politicians should get out of the way and let people with real educational expertise run our schools. If this happens, things can only get better.

# References

Hartocollis, Anemona. New SAT Has More Reading (Even in Math) and More Fretting, *The New York Times,* February 9, 2016. http://nyti.ms/1Qqq1ST.

Colleges and Universities That Do Not Use SAT/ACT Scores for Admitting Substantial Numbers of Students Into Bachelor Degree Programs. *National Center for Fair and Open Testing.* Winter 2016. http://bit.ly/1TYHHYj.

Taylor, Kate. 92 New York City High Schools to Give No-Fee SAT On Saturday, *The New York Times,* March 2, 2016. http://nyti. ms/1RMG2Dg.

Zhang, Zara Study Finds High School GPA Trumps SAT in Predicting College Success, *The Harvard Crimson Admissions Blog,* March 3, 2014 http://bit.ly/1QqnoR2.

# CHAPTER 16

# Forging Strong Relationships With Students Should Be Top Of Your To-Do List.

*"Never* let your ego get in the way when dealing with children who are misbehaving." -Dr. Doug Green

AS TEACHERS START a new school year, many will be armed with long to-do lists of all the things they hope to achieve over the coming months. Very near the top of that list should be something on which almost all success will hinge – forming the strongest possible relationships you can with students.

In his book, *You've Gotta Connect: Building Relationships that Lead to Engaged Students, Productive Classrooms, and Higher Achievement*, James Alan Sturtevant makes the case that the most important thing teachers can do is connect with and accept their students. It may not always be easy, but once you do connect, students will behave better and learn more.

As I surf the Internet every day to do my blog at http://DrDougGreen. Com, I continue to find many other experienced educators saying the same thing. I would go so far as to say that there is a consensus that the most important thing that teachers can do is work on forming strong working relationships with their students.

## You Need a Relationship Plan

As you prepare for the new semester, try to have a plan for how to best relate to and empathize with your class. Surveys for students and parents are something you can have ready for day one. Forging relationships with parents may not be easy. Not all will respond to surveys and questionnaires. But an early display that you are interested in their son or daughter; asking them what they think you should know about them; finding out what their child likes or dislikes about school and what they do outside of school hours will help. It will also help you learn about their expectations of you as a teacher.

Student surveys will vary by grade level, but in any case, you need to find out what they are interested in and what they like and don't like about school. Consider asking them what they liked the most about their favorite teacher.

## Get Help From Administration

If you have time and cooperation from administration, you can go beyond planning what to do when school starts. With class list(s) in hand, you can start to learn students' names. Ideally you will have access to student information like previous grades, teacher comments, test scores, and perhaps a recent photograph.

If you can access food service information, you will know which students qualify for free or reduced meals. Unfortunately, the stresses that come with poverty often result in these kids having more in the way of academic and behavior issues. This means that you may want to work on those relationships first. Since poverty is not evenly distributed, some teachers will have all students from disadvantaged homes while others will have few or none.

For more on this see my summary of Eric Jensen's *Teaching with Poverty in Mind: What Being Poor Does to Kids' Brains and What Schools Can Do About It. http://bit.ly/2f5BppN.* Also check out his other book on the subject *Engaging Students with Poverty in Mind: Practical Strategies for Raising Achievement.*

Take a look at student addresses to find out where they live. If you aren't familiar with their neighborhood, hit the road and see what it's like where they live. This may not work for everyone, but try to walk their streets if you can. You may run into some former students and parents who can help you get to know the incoming crop. Knowing where they live will also provide fodder for conversations that can build relationships.

This kind of effort is more practical for elementary teachers who only have twenty-five students or so with whom to develop relationships. For secondary teachers, this process is much more daunting as they are likely to have one hundred students or more. In this case I recommend that you gather your class lists and book a meeting with administrators.

The goal here is to learn what they know about the students they know best. They are likely to be students with discipline issues. These will be the students that you want to focus on first since students who have good relationships with their teachers are less likely to act badly in your class.

As principal I saw many students who had discipline problems with one teacher and did just fine with other teachers. In most cases the problems were a result of the teacher treating the student with disdain rather than respect. You can be respectful even if you have to let a student know that he or she has to change a negative behavior.

Certainly, teachers who had your incoming students will know more than administrators in most cases. Reach out to them when you can. Anything they can tell you should help with relationship building.

## A Fresh Start is Essential

I always believed in giving even the most difficult students a fresh start, but it helps to know as much as you can going in. This will allow you to have high yet appropriate expectations for all of the young people who you will soon know and care for. As principal I also met with the middle school principal who would inherit my fifth graders in the fall.

As I have indicated before, the real key is respect. It is vital to treat all students with respect even when they don't deserve it. A wise special education teacher who dealt daily with emotionally disturbed students once told me, "Dr. Green, be sure to let the other teachers know that they should *never* let their ego get into it when dealing with children who are misbehaving." This is probably the best single piece of advice that I was ever given by another educator.

I'll end with a story that makes my point here. Toward the end of my career as an elementary principal, I had several administrative interns. I tried to give them real work to do and always assigned them to supervise our eight buses at dismissal. I was always out with them, but stood back unless I was needed.

One day an intern named Corey came to me and said there was a fifth grade student causing a disruption on the first bus, which was blocking all the other buses. He said he tried to settle the kid down but had no luck. I told him that I would deal with it.

I entered the bus and approached the student, quietly calling him by his first name. I said in a calm respectful voice "Thomas, we really need to get this bus moving. Would you be so kind as to take a seat so that can happen?" The student sat peacefully and the buses left. When I exited the bus Corey came up to me and asked "How the hell did you do that?" I simply told him, "Corey, I have a relationship with Thomas." That's all it took. I'm happy to say that Corey is now a successful superintendent.

I'm sure some administrators would have taken Thomas off of the bus and suspended him. I'm convinced that there would be fewer suspensions and more academic success if only *all* educators used constant respect as the foundation to building strong working relationships.

# References

Jensen, Eric (2013). *Engaging Students with Poverty in Mind: Practical Strategies for Raising Achievement,* ASCD: Alexandria, VA.

Jensen, Eric (2009). *Teaching with Poverty in Mind: What Being Poor Does to Kids' Brains and What Schools Can Do About It,* ASCD: Alexandria, VA.

Sturtevant, James Allan. *You've Gotta Connect: Building Relationships that Lead to Engaged Students, Productive Classrooms, and Higher Achievement,* 2014, World Book: Chicago, IL.

# CHAPTER 17

# Good Luck Learning a Foreign Language in American Schools

"There is little evidence that many students achieve much fluency in high school." -Jay Mathews, Washington Post

AS A FRESHMAN in high school I took French I, and after earning a 75, I trudged on to French II. The French II teacher spoke French most of the time and I didn't understand much. I decided to get a fresh start with German I. Somehow I slogged through two years of a language that was at least easier to spell, but featured three definite articles rather than two. Yet again I earned the lowest grades of my high school career.

In college I majored in Chemistry, which required a year of German. I earned a pair of C's and was thrilled to see it in the rear-view mirror. The next time I had to deal with a foreign language was during my Army basic combat training during the Viet Nam era. As part of initial processing we took a foreign language aptitude test. To my surprise, my grade indicated that I had a high aptitude for learning a foreign language, something my high school teachers missed.

# Hello, Sweden

In 1980 I took my mother to visit her relatives in Sweden with whom she had been corresponding since World War II. While Swedish was my mother's first language, the only words I learned from her were a few curse words. To prepare for the trip, my wife and I got some Berlitz tapes and listened as often as possible. This allowed us to learn the basics so we could engage in basic communication with my mother's older relatives who didn't speak English.

We found that communicating at the dinner table was a tiring experience, but by pointing and asking simple questions like 'what do you call that?' and 'how much does that cost?' we got by. In the process, it wasn't long before I was able to put sentences together that were understood, and the compliments followed. It seems that I did have a good aptitude for learning another language.

How was it that my efforts in French and German class in high school were futile while my independent efforts to learn Swedish were successful? My first guess was that in Sweden I was immersed, there was a rich context for all language use, and I was very motivated. All of these things were missing at my high school.

# Enter the Refugees

As principal of Woodrow Wilson Elementary in Binghamton, New York, 25% of my students were refugees who arrived knowing little English. I got to see kids come in with no English and leave fairly fluent. It was also obvious to me that the younger students learned faster than their older siblings. Research supports this. (I should also note that the refugees were my best students when it came to effort and behavior.)

According to Jay Mathews, the education columnist for the Washington Post, "There is little evidence that many students achieve much fluency in high school." The problem has something to do with the artificial way languages are presented in schools. Typically, students spend a period of forty minutes each day dealing with the second language, while all other classes are English only. My foreign language teachers also assumed that I had mastered English grammar, which I hadn't.

My refugees were immersed in a sea of English all day. This explains part of why they learned so fast. It also explains my success with Swedish. Television shows in Sweden were either in Swedish or in English with Swedish subtitles. I found both types to be very powerful learning experiences.

## Why Is It So Difficult For English Speakers?

English speakers often bemoan the fact that we are poor at learning other languages. This shouldn't be a surprise. It's the rare school that starts students on a second language prior to the age of twelve. Research indicates that with puberty comes increased difficulty in learning languages. In other words, schools in the U.S. wait until it's too late for kids to have an easier time learning a second language.

It isn't hard to find research to support this as in this from the blog of a Penn State course:

> For a child, learning language is part of their brain chemistry. They are literally built to absorb information; they do this in an unconscious state of mind, like they're learning and they don't even know it. Adults and older children, on the other hand, have to consciously learn the information, which makes it harder.

One situation at my school was very telling. I had a family arrive from Iraq with kids in kindergarten, 2nd, 3rd, and 5th grade. The 5th grader could fluently read and write Arabic and was clearly rather intelligent. After several months, it was clear that the kindergartener was significantly ahead of his older brother and was even helping him learn English.

In Sweden, students start English in the 3rd grade. Students in foreign countries may have parents who speak English. I've seen this up close visiting homes in Quebec, France, and Sweden. There are English speakers all over the world, which makes it easier for English speakers to travel without making an effort to learn the local language. Natives also often want to practice their English on you.

Consider the world's media. In most other countries, pop stars sing in English and the world's most popular movies are originally voiced in English. As you travel the world, you will be exposed to a lot of English media.

I'm convinced, however, that the most important issue is motivation. In high school and college, I had no motivation for learning another language. The only motivation for most students in the U.S. is getting good grades or just getting by. When it was time to visit my Swedish-speaking relatives, however, I was motivated. Research supports the importance of motivation when it comes to learning anything.

Non-English speakers also know that opportunities will vastly expand if they become fluent in English. The only jobs in most countries that don't require English are low-level manufacturing or other kinds of labor. In Sweden, for example, you can be a lumberjack without learning English, but not much else.

## So What Should We Do?

According to Professor John McWhorter in his Great Course *The Story of Human Language*, Chinese and Arabic are not single languages but families of languages. While the Mandarin version of Chinese is the most common, it won't be that helpful if you travel to places like Canton, Shanghai, and Taiwan.

While written Arabic is understood around the Arab world, spoken Arabic in one country or tribe is likely to be hard to follow in another country or tribe. This tells me that taking either language in high school may not be that useful. These languages are probably better suited to intensive courses like those used in the military.

After English, Spanish is the most common language in the world. In many parts of the U.S., a knowledge of Spanish can be useful. If you travel south of the border, Spanish will help just about anywhere other than Brazil. Spain itself is also a popular tourist destination.

If you have some reason to visit Québec, France, some islands in the Caribbean or some countries in Africa, French could be handy. As for other languages, they are not commonly taught in schools so you might be on your own with resources from the Internet and smart phone apps like us Swedish learners.

I doubt many schools in the U.S. will move language instruction to elementary schools, and I'm not sure they should. The cost of bringing in language specialists would not produce the desired results since the students would just get a brief exposure and again would probably lack motivation, context, or immersion.

## Enter the Parents

It is probably up to parents to make real fluency happen. If parents know another language, they should use it around the house as often as possible. If they have some motivation to learn another language themselves, they should include their children in the process. Also look for opportunities to go to places where only the other language is allowed.

A semester abroad is often an opportunity for older students. However, if a student is placed in a home where the family wants to practice their English, they might not learn much. Look for a placement in a small town where English is not as common and there are parents or some family members such as young children who don't speak English. The attitude of the student is probably the most important variable here.

When my three-year-old daughter visited my Swedish cousins, she spent time with my cousin's three older children who were studying English at school. They liked playing with her as it allowed them to practice their English. Look for such opportunities for your kids. Also look for children's media in the target language. To this day, I like to watch children's programs in French and Swedish.

For many poor parents English is a second language. Let them know that they should help their kids learn their native language. Tell them the effort is worth it as learning another language has been shown to be good for one's brain. Students who hear another language at home should take that language in school if they can. Some poor kids in this situation might enjoy a lot more success than usual if they do this.

Wealthy parents often hire childcare workers whose first language is not English. If you are in this demographic, tell the caregiver to talk to your child in their first language as well as English.

Going from one subject for forty minutes to another to another doesn't seem to me to be the best way to learn anything. This approach is even less effective for foreign languages. Perhaps online self-paced courses with lots of media could do a better job. It may not address the motivation issue, but it could provide a richer context. Since we know that the traditional approach isn't working, it's time to at least try something else. Also, be sure to order a few cases of motivation.

## Resources

Alban, Deane. The Brain Benefits of Learning a Second Language, *Be Brain Fit*. Downloaded May 25, 2017, http://bit.ly/2qTxVPy

Edmonds, Molly. What's the best age to learn a new language? *How Stuff Works Culture*, Downloaded May 25, 2017, http://bit.ly/2qTsaSd.

Learning a Second Language Is Easier for Children, But Why? The course website and blog for the Fall 2014 semester of Penn State's SC200 course, http://bit.ly/2qTsy2Z.

Mathews, Jay. Why waste time on a foreign language?, *The Washington Post*, April 22, 2014, http://wapo.st/2qToXSw.

McWhorter, John. The Story of Human Language, 2004, *The Teaching Company*, Audible original recording.

Oroujlou, Nasser. Motivation, attitude, and language learning, *Science Direct*, Volume 29, 2011, Pages 994-1000, http://bit.ly/2qT7QjG.

# CHAPTER 18

# The Arts: One More Victim of Common Core Testing

"The lesson for all schools is if you want to get parents into your school, put their kids on stage or feed them." -Dr. Doug Green

EVERYWHERE YOU LOOK there are the arts, and their huge capacity to add value to our lives is something schools need to better understand. Like many, I am convinced that the standardized testing that resulted from NCLB legislation and Obama's Race to The Top has done significant harm to our educational system, the students it serves, and the arts in general.

Here I take a look, not only at its impact on the arts, but also some practices that schools commonly use and how I think they can be changed for the better. By the arts, I'm referring to music, art, drama, and dance as they are taught in schools.

Since standardized testing began in earnest in the 1990s, there has been pressure to spend more of the school day on the subjects being tested. From what I have seen, just about every district has increased lessons dealing with math and English language arts. In most schools the cost of extending the school day for such lessons is prohibitive so the extra math and ELA time has had to come at the cost of other subjects.

Certainly the arts have taken some of these cuts, along with subjects like science, social studies, and physical education. In the school where I was principal, music was cut from twice a week to once every six days, which is a 60% cut. Art was only cut by 20% but it still took a significant hit and a class only occurs every sixth day. I haven't seen a national study that details the average cutbacks for schools, but it is easy to find articles that focus on specific schools like mine.

Since much of the music program in a school falls into the extracurricular arena, it also tends to be a much bigger target for budget cuts in general. In New York State, for example, districts are generally limited to a 2% increase in their local tax levy each year unless they get permission from 60% of the voters to go higher. The drama and dance programs are also hit for the same reason.

## How Music Education Should Change

As an amateur musician, I have a fairly good idea about this. I earned a varsity chorus letter in high school (please don't laugh too hard), earned tuition money in college playing in a rock band, and have been a member of a number of church and community choirs since.

As principal I played and sang for assemblies and for smaller groups. I still perform for school groups and do guest appearances in churches. My father played piano for a dance band in the 1920s and 30s so I guess I got my music gene from him.

In 1952 I began my music career thanks to a kindergarten activity called rhythm band. I don't recall how often we did this during our half-day session, but it was far and away my favorite activity. The teacher passed out a rhythm instrument of some sort to each student and led the band by singing and/or playing the piano.

In the last twenty years I have visited kindergartens in many schools and I have yet to see one with rhythm band in the curriculum. I think it's time to bring it back. The instruments would be inexpensive but the teachers would need some musical skill. Perhaps the most musical kindergarten teacher in the school could do this activity with all kindergarten classes. This activity could also introduce language, social studies, and science concepts.

Over the years I have seen the work of many wonderful music teachers. I've seen schools with class sets of pianos and guitars and even one school with a class set of steel drums. Not only are the concerts great entertainment, but they also do a great job of pulling parents and other community members into the school. The lesson for all schools is, if you want to get parents into your school, put their kids on stage. I also found that I could get parents to come to school by offering food along with some other activity.

## Do What I Say, When I Say, and How I Say

If there is a downside to what music teachers do, it can be traced to the fact that when they lead a group, they are referred to as directors. What they essentially do is tell all students what to do, how to do it, and when to do it. This leaves little or no room for innovation or creativity on the part of the students. This is true to a lesser extent in sports where students have to do a lot of their own thinking once the game starts.

Some music teachers do, however, allow for creativity on behalf of the students. At just about any level you can challenge students to make up lyrics to a given melody and/or melodies of their own. This can support the ELA effort, as can reading lyrics while singing.

After they learn a bit about musical notation, you can ask them to write their own songs. At some point you can expect them to add harmonies. I suspect that students with better musical aptitude will go beyond class expectations and write more original music. They can also make videos of their work and post them on YouTube.

I've even seen some music directors use student-created work as performance pieces for school groups. Another place in which students commonly improvise is the student jazz band. If your school has one or more of these groups be sure that the students create their own solo parts and look for opportunities to let students direct student performing groups.

## The Poverty Problem

Another problem the music program faces is growing participation with children who lack parental support and resources. Many performing groups have rehearsals in the evening and performances on nights and weekends. This almost always requires parents to get their children to school and pick them up. In my district most poor parents didn't have cars and lived too far from the school to walk.

While voices are free, instrumental groups often require the rental or purchase of instruments. Wealthier parents also routinely pay for private lessons to supplement what the school music teacher can do. Even though most band directors can play every instrument, there will be some instruments on which they have only rudimentary skill. This was the case for my daughter, who played French horn. Without private lessons there was no chance that she would make the select band or the regional orchestra.

This problem became obvious to me the first time I attended a middle school concert in which my daughter played. At that time I was principal of a high poverty elementary school and my students fed into the same middle school as the elementary school my daughter attended. My school had a high minority and refugee population so our performing groups looked like a meeting at the United Nations.

When I scanned the performing groups at the middle school, it was easy to see that only Whites and Asians were included, and that almost all of the participants were from the wealthier schools. That prompted me to start my own little bus service to transport a car full of minority kids to evening rehearsals.

## Art for Art's Sake

I was a K-5 principal from 1993 until 2006. When I started, kindergarten was mostly structured play and socialization with some time devoted to letter and number recognition, learning a few sight words, and simple math operations. There was also a lot of art time.

Now if you visit a kindergarten, it will seem a lot more like what first grade looked like in 1993. (See an earlier chapter on this topic.) It seems that many school leaders have reasoned that if they push more reading and math lessons into kindergarten it will somehow translate into better test scores once the students get to third grade. This has resulted in a big reduction in the amount of time kindergarten students spend drawing, painting, cutting, pasting, and doing other things artistic.

The people who argue against pushing more reading and math into kindergarten believe that students need to reach a certain developmental level before such lessons can be effective. Trying to teach a student something they are not ready to learn only causes frustration for students and teachers alike.

My fear is that many more students will begin to dislike school in kindergarten. In addition to less art in kindergarten, I've seen the same trend from the first grade on. What I don't get is how taking away crayons and markers from students and giving them number two pencils is a good idea. It's like we are trying to make school more boring on purpose.

As it is with other subjects, some students are naturally more artistic than others. How much is genetic and how much is due to resources at home is anyone's guess, but most people think that both are in play. I was never very artistic, but my daughter was a stand-out artist as early as kindergarten. She also stated clearly at age five that she wanted to make cartoons when she grew up. Fortunately, her mother and I had the vision to support whatever she was interested in. This required some learning on our part but we must have done something right as she is now a working, non-starving artist in New York City.

My advice is to go back to the future when it comes to art and play in kindergarten. I would even allow naps as needed, unlike the old days when everyone had to nap at the same time even if they weren't tired. I'm sure some students would go all day in kindergarten without a nap.

Ideally naps could be possible for kids in all grades just like they are in many innovative businesses. As for art activities, try to allow for as much creativity as possible and avoid the type of step-by-step projects where everyone's efforts look pretty much the same.

For grades above kindergarten, I would like to see more opportunities for students to illustrate assignments and make things. The maker movement that is being pushed in many innovative schools is something I believe that all schools should adopt.

The good news for students who are less artistically skilled is that modern technology makes photography and videography available, easy, and inexpensive. Any kid can make photos and videos. New technology such as 3D printers can also allow less artistic students to make things.

There is no reason why student writing projects can't include illustrations and/or photographs. There should also be opportunities for students to write scripts for videos that they then create either as individuals or teams. Here is just one more example of how the arts can integrate ELA.

## High School and Beyond

One thing I don't want to see are high school courses designed to teach specific software packages. Many high schools have courses for artistic applications like Adobe's Photoshop and Illustrator. When my daughter went through high school, the art department didn't have computers. This meant they taught her art rather than software. I realized, of course, that she would have to learn Photoshop among other applications so I signed her up for a self-paced online course that she finished in four weeks on her own.

One of the problems I see with education is that every body of knowledge gets somehow crammed into the sacred semester. Did I miss the part in the Bible where on the eighth day God created the semester and saw that it was good? It certainly isn't necessary for learning software. This looks like an ideal and easy way to bring online blended learning to any school if the teachers' unions will cooperate.

As someone who bought his first personal computer in 1979, I pretty much had to teach myself the software packages I wanted to use in addition to writing my own programs. When I bought the first

Macintosh in 1984, I entered the world of pull down menus. This invention made learning much easier, as you can search the menus until you find the item that you want to do.

If a student can learn software on their own, how about we just get out of their way? If they feel like they need help, this is where self-paced online courses are ideal. This doesn't mean that they can't go to a teacher or another student for help.

## A Word About Drama and Dance

These subjects are generally relegated to the last year or two of high school. Drama classes are usually English electives and dance classes are not taught at all in many, if not most, high schools. A big part of many high school cultures are the yearly musical performances that fill school auditoriums for several nights and make temporary stars out of a few students. This is where students learn acting and dancing sort of on the fly after school. A high level of motivation certainly helps.

Early in my career I was the technical director for the drama program at the 7-12 secondary school where I worked (Cortland, New York). It was my job to round up students who wanted to design, build, and change sets, and design and operate lighting and sound equipment. This was pretty cool as it allowed students to be creative and perhaps more importantly to collaborate. For the most part I just saw to it that they had the supplies and equipment they needed and stayed out of their way.

The creativity and collaboration also extended to the actors since they had to create their characters and work together. Many cast members were called upon to dance and for some, at least the boys, this represented their first formal dance instruction. Members of the pit band had less in the way of creative experiences, but they certainly got to polish their playing skills beyond what would happen without these musical opportunities. Pit bands also included adults as mentors.

Unfortunately, these shows require nighttime rehearsals at least during the weeks prior to the show, and for kids without parental support, their opportunities to participate are at risk. Students with more means and support are also much more likely to take private dance and acting lessons. Look around and you will no doubt see a number of private dance studios where you live.

The bottom line is that these performances involve a lot of students in activities that may be more valuable in the long run than what they experience in their classes. I believe that they also give a positive boost to the school's culture and climate. I would encourage schools to look for ways to expand this type of activity. Classes could conceivably create and perform their own plays and musicals. Perhaps multiple student one acts or short skits would work as a student production. Student-made videos can also fit here and they can be easily shared with the world via YouTube.

## Real World Here We Come - The Artsy Job Market

What most parents want out of school for their students is a decent shot at good job. I suspect many worry that majoring in one of the arts disciplines does not result in great chances for well-paid steady work. When you look at the job market, it varies greatly from one discipline to another. I think that it's safe to say that there are more art jobs than jobs for musicians, dancers, and actors.

I'm somewhat familiar with this job market since my daughter is part of it. She went to art school (Pratt Institute in Brooklyn, New York) and when she graduated in 2006, she got a good job immediately and has been working ever since. As an art major, she took several studio courses each semester, which required many hours in the studio polishing her skills every day. The professors also gave honest and helpful critiques during each session. Keep in mind that it is hard to improve if you don't get feedback from someone with expertise. After four years of this, you should be ready to make real art for someone.

Art jobs require you to do what the boss wants rather than engaging in your own thing. In other words, during the day you are "working for the man." If you aren't willing to do this, you just might find yourself in the starving artist niche. Even if you work for someone else during the day, you can make your own art after hours, and from what I have seen, most artists do. If you are wondering what kind of jobs are out there, just take a look at television shows, publications of all kinds, computer games, and just about anything on the Internet.

Any illustrations, photos, videos, and animations you see were created by an artist or more likely, a team of artists. There are lots of different art majors, and some are more likely to lead to good jobs than others. Search the http://GlassDorr.Com site to see currently available jobs with locations and starting salaries.

Do your homework. Also consider going to the best school you can get into in a big city where getting good internships is easier. This is where you meet real people in the industry and expand your network. Some schools like Pratt also let you work on a teaching certificate at the same time as a backup plan. I should also note that some schools in smaller cities do a good job of getting internships in cities not near the campus.

## Music for Moolah

For musicians the job market is not as good. Even many top jobs in symphony orchestras are part time, so you will have to cobble together additional work such as giving private lessons. A back up teaching certificate is probably more important here. There are jobs for bands playing popular music, but it's hard to make a living wage playing a few nights a week. Band jobs have also decreased from the time when I played in a band in college thanks to the rise of the DJ and singers who sing to recorded music.

For singers the chances are even more bleak. There are hardly any paid choir jobs and not many paid jobs for professional singers at local opera houses. Unless you are really good and persistent, you will need a plan B. There are outliers like Taylor Swift and Katie Perry of course, but chances for those kind of jobs are far greater than one in million. Acting jobs exist in most communities, but those jobs are part time and end when the show ends. Even movie stars are often unemployed when a film ends, and like music, true stardom is rare.

Dancers have the same problems as actors and musicians with one more problem of their own. Dancers are essentially athletes whose careers are limited in duration thanks to the aging process. While it is possible to dance into your 50s and beyond, don't expect to find a lot of work. Unlike art music and drama, even teaching jobs are rare for dancers unless you want to open your own studio.

Many non-art occupations have artistic aspects so don't think you only need knowledge of the arts if you pursue an art-specific job. For example, architects need to be good at engineering and design. People who deal with communications and media run into music, drama, dance, and art at every turn. English majors often get involved in writing scripts for some kind of productions. Interior designers, landscapers, woodworkers, camp counselors, and many others work with artistic concepts daily, and the list goes on.

## Adding Value for Life

Even if you find that your day job is totally devoid of artistic features, the arts can certainly add value to your life in many ways. I find that playing one of my instruments is very therapeutic. It's like the rest of the world goes away while you are playing. I also get a big kick out of playing for others as an amateur in churches, schools, and parks. Even if you didn't begin playing in school, it is possible to start at almost any age.

The same is true for the other arts. While taking my daughter to art classes when she was a child, I saw that the classes often contained adults who were just getting started. My mother-in-law even joined a senior citizen dance group (the Happy Hoofers) well into her 70s that performed at nursing homes and marched in parades. Local drama groups usually have roles for actors and singers of every age.

Even if you don't choose to participate in the arts, you can certainly enjoy them as a spectator. Where I live there are several performances of various kinds almost every week that are usually inexpensive or free. I'm also a big fan of museums—particularly those that seem to attract more visitors every year. This is in addition to the countless opportunities available on television and online.

It seems like it is the rare person who doesn't enjoy some kind of music and artistic performance. It would indeed be a less enjoyable life without our nearly constant exposure to the arts. I also find that as I gain a more sophisticated understanding of an art form, I enjoy it even more. (See my chapter on Opera near the end of this book.)

## In Conclusion

My advice for education's leaders is to look for more ways to integrate the arts into English Language Arts activities and other subjects at all grades. If you have cut time for the arts for more test prep, at least go back to what you had prior to those cuts. If you do these two things there will be more arts in your school, not less. I suspect that most students will find school more enjoyable and be more motivated to learn and create something.

If students use language as they create songs, skits, and plays, I suspect that they will do at least as well if not better on standardized tests. If, as I hope, states start to pare back or eliminate tests, your school will be ahead of the game when it comes to heading back to the future.

I would also reach out to parents and let them know what is going on in the local artistic community so they can involve their children. Over the years I took my daughter to every museum and performance that I could, and I'm sure it made a difference. For schools with poor children, there should be a focus on art-oriented field trips and bringing in as many artists as possible. Some like me, for example, will even come in for free.

## References

Douglas, Katherine M and Jaquith, Diane B. Engaging Learners Through Artmaking: Choice-Based Art Education in the Classroom 1st Edition, (2009). *Teachers College, Teachers College Press*: New York, NY.

Moomaw, Sally (2002). More Than Singing: Discovering Music in Preschool and Kindergarten, Self Published Book, http://amzn.to/2qyQzsw

Sackstein, Starr. Revisions to the Draft Require Parent Input, *Education Week Teacher*, August 4, 2014.

Sackstein, Starr. What I learned from Chorus, *Education Week Teacher*, March 23, 2015.

# CHAPTER 19

# Teachers/Parents: Don't Run Away from Discussing Porn.

"Never before has so much indecent material been so easily accessible to so many minors." -U. S. Department of Justice

"With young people accessing more explicit material online than ever, teachers have a responsibility to protect students. This won't happen if they avoid the subject." -Dr. Doug Green

WHEN I WAS growing up, my sex education came by way of magazines like *Playboy* and whatever my friends gleaned from their older siblings. Sex education in schools today varies radically. Some push abstinence until marriage and others explain how the plumbing works, along with birth control and STDs. I'm not familiar, however, with any that discuss Internet porn, but the reality is that the majority of students today are getting a great deal of their sex education via action-packed videos on the Internet as many schools and parents look the other way.

According to a U.S. Department of Justice report "never before has so much indecent material been so easily accessible to so many minors." While schools do a good job blocking adult sites, many

TEACHING ISN'T ROCKET SCIENCE, IT'S WAY MORE COMPLEX

parents do not and kids are skilled at working around blocking software. They can also access porn on their smart phones just about anywhere.

Young people who try to copy what they see on the Internet put themselves at risk. In the past, when new sources of risk such as drugs or sexually transmitted diseases entered our culture, teachers were quick to add warnings to their lesson plans due to their concern and feeling of responsibility for their students.

Sadly, this doesn't seem to be happening with pornography. The bottom line is that while it might be difficult to talk about, teachers must not run away from discussing porn, be it via the Internet or other sources. This topic would fit naturally into health classes in middle school and high school, along with current sex education and warnings about other risky behaviors. It could come up in other classes as well so all teachers should be ready.

Start by letting students know that interest in this material is normal. Lack of interest is also normal. If you have watched it, you are not a pervert and should not feel guilty. Let them know that research indicates that some students in the class have seen it and some haven't, and that they shouldn't be judged by which group they are in.

## What to Discuss

Discuss that these videos feature actors rather than people in love who are making love. Note that some of the material contains acts that can be dangerous. Talk about consent. When a partner says no, respect it. Make them aware that making their own videos of themselves and their under-aged friends can result in arrest for making and possessing child pornography. Also cover the concept of *Revenge Porn*. This happens when girls send boyfriends revealing photos or videos and then they become ex-boyfriends (and vice versa).

While the life of a porn star may seem glamorous to some young people, porn stars are much more likely to abuse drugs, contract sexually transmitted diseases, and earn little money in the long run. Discuss the realities with your class. Such conversations should happen after you get to know your students so your own knowledge and judgment can come into play.

Prior to broaching this topic, some parental outreach should occur. I recommend that the district form a committee to determine how and where these conversations should fit into the curriculum. Try to have several parents on this committee. Having parental involvement should help if other parents complain. Be sure to give all parents the main principles you will touch on. Also, encourage them to have similar conversations at home and to encourage honesty and lack of consequences.

If you inform all parents ahead of time, you can also give them the choice to opt their kids out of these lessons. If your school isn't ready for such conversations in the classroom, it must at least try to get the parents started. If, like most schools, leadership is looking the other way in regard to this topic, do what you can to get the conversation started. This is not a conversation that teachers should be running away from.

## What is Really Out There?

WARNING: this section contains some graphic content.

Finding porn on the Internet couldn't be easier. I suspect that most of my readers can even guess the names of some popular porn sites. How about Sex.Com? Yep. Rather than YouTube, would you suspect something like PornTube? If so, you wouldn't be disappointed. There is also PornHub, YouPorn, XMovies, and many others, most of which are owned by the same company. There is also a site called XHamster. Com. Guess what kids would find if they searched innocently on hamster and videos. That's right, this porn site is at the top of the list.

How is it that a retired educator knows enough about Internet porn to inform others as to what it offers so that they don't have to go there? It started in 1996 when the elementary school where I was principal got Internet workstations in each classroom. I soon received a call from a fourth grade class where the students had searched for

"Spice Girls" and saw some spicy pictures. They were a popular group that featured five young attractive British female singers. The Internet already had nude pictures of some of the Spice Girls. In addition, some early porn sites used the term to attract viewers.

That prompted me to start helping our district tech support team more effectively block adult content. For a month or so, I tried to break through the blocking software. When I succeeded, I told the tech staff. In the process, I got a look at how the adult industry was using the Internet just as it has used every other previous new medium from cave paintings on. Schools in general have come a long way in regard to blocking inappropriate content, and, if anything, many block too much—including sites such as Twitter and YouTube.

Surveys show that most teens and even some pre-teens are viewing Internet porn at homes and places where the public has Internet access. Although some students accidentally view porn while surfing, the majority are looking for it. A simple search of the word porn offers dozens of sites offering free explicit videos. While some sites feature a home page with a warning and buttons to click on if you are not 18+ or don't wish to view adult material, most don't. Many home pages feature a grid of thumbnail pictures taken from the videos with titles that imply what the scene is about. There is also a button marked 'categories' at the top where you can click to see the specific kind of action you are interested in.

Pornhub.Com, for example, has no less than 86 categories. In other words, something for everyone. The most popular categories include teens, oral sex, masturbation, lesbians, bondage, spanking, big boobs, small boobs, gay men, transgender, public nudity, gang bangs, spanking, and anal sex. Video clips vary in length from a minute or two to over an hour, and in quality from home made cellphone clips to professionally made material. You can spot the professional content as it has professional lighting.

All sites that offer free material feature advertising and try to get you to pay for premium access that gives you longer and better quality videos. Enterprising women also set up their own personal sites where they charge a monthly fee for access to all content. You will even find that some young girls are making money from their bedrooms or dorm rooms by using web cams to capture their performances for pay. Live cams are also popular. This lets you see a live performance while talking to the actor(s).

Professional sites require that actors prove they are at least eighteen, but don't be surprised if you see girls who don't look that old, as they are in high demand. I'm happy to say that I have yet to run across anything that looks like child pornography, but you know it's out there somewhere. Also, if you want to see pubic hair you may need to go to the "hairy" category. You would think it was outlawed in the 1990s.

## What Will Boys Expect Girls to Do

When I looked at my *Playboy* magazines in the 1950s, I learned what women looked like naked, but had no idea what to do if I found myself with a naked girl. Thanks to the Internet, all the wondering is over. With Internet porn as a primer, young men, and women, will certainly know what to do with a great deal of variation.

For parents of young girls, I recommend Peggy Orenstein's book *Girls and Sex: Navigating the Complicated New Landscape.* You can start by reading my summary at Dr. Doug Green.com http://bit.ly/2hEyWDC. Peggy interviewed over 70 girls between the age of 15 and 22 and scoured the research on this subject. This book makes it clear that boys' expectations aren't what they were prior to the introduction of Internet porn.

In my day, oral sex was something couples usually engaged in after they were married if they did it at all. Today, oral sex is the new third base in that it often happens prior to intercourse. Boys are likely to expect it and pressure girls to do it shortly after couples start making out. Boys are also less likely to return the favor but some do.

Anal sex is fairly common on the Internet. Peggy's conversations, however, indicate that it is often painful and can cause bleeding. The message for girls is don't be surprised if your boyfriend expects you to give it a try as it is now known as the new *5th base.*

Girls should also expect their boyfriend to ask about pubic hair removal as it's the rare video that features a woman with a full complement of genital hair. Many women have no pubic hair while some have a small patch just above the clitorus, affectionately known as a landing strip. Girls can choose between waxing and shaving and many will take the initiative before the boys say anything.

Many men in these videos have also shed their pubic hair as it is probably the only way to make one's penis appear longer, and many women also prefer it. Local beauty parlors now offer pubic hair removal beyond the traditional bikini wax. The shop that provides this service in my town is called the Pretty Kitty. You can also find ads for Brazilians, which feature total hair removal. Men can go there too and get boyzilians. Now there is a word my spell checker hasn't seen yet.

## Porn Induced Erectile Dysfunction

Recent research shows an alarming increase in erectile dysfunction among men under forty, including teens. The prominent theory among researchers is that boys and men who spend a lot of time having solo sex with the help of Internet porn are having difficulty getting aroused when in the presence of a real naked female.

According to a 2013 study in the *Journal of Sexual Medicine*, nearly one out of four new erectile dysfunction patients is under the age of forty – a surprising finding, given that erectile dysfunction has traditionally been thought of as an affliction of men in their sixties and seventies.

In his TED Talk, Gary Wilson argues that as the brain creates more and more dopamine, it tires out, prompting a need for increasingly more frequent and intense stimulation. If a man masturbates to porn too frequently, by age 22 or so, a guy's sexual taste can be like deep roots in his brain. As they watch porn that gets increasingly more hardcore and aggressive, it may lead men to seek out porn that is more and more "extreme." The only solution? To quit masturbating to porn entirely. Once that happens, Wilson explains, "his taste can revert" back to normal, because "brains are plastic."

Not all researchers are on the same page with this matter. Sex therapist, Ian Kerner, who treats many young men with erectile dysfunction, says that anecdotally, he has seen a slight increase in young male situational ED cases. Yet he says that the link between porn and erectile dysfunction is "more correlative than causal." Kerner lists performance anxiety, internalized sexual shame, or intimacy issues as possible culprits as well, particularly as hookup apps create more opportunities for casual sex.

In his book *The Butterfly Effect*, Jon Ronson points out that the increase in ED in young men began to increase rapidly once high bandwidth video streaming became widely available in 2008. This was the same time that a company in Montreal started PornHub that featured an almost unlimited access to free adult video clips. This not only changed the behavior of many men and some women, it also had a profound impact on the porn business itself. It isn't unusual for published porn to be available free online shortly after it is published. People who looked forward to getting rich in this business are now finding it difficult to just get by.

As he researched this book, Ronson interviewed a wide variety of people in the industry and their customers. If you want to learn about how access to limitless adult content has changed our culture, this book will help. He even points out that Internet porn has caused one job to disappear. Before male actors could access porn videos on their cell phones, porn producers hired women called fluffers to help men achieve erections before they started their scenes. Now the guys just use their cell phones even though there is often a naked real female in the room.

## Girls Gone Wild

Another genre that could impact young women features the Girls Gone Wild and related videos. These videos are shot on location at Mardi Gras events and similar wild street parties. They feature girls being asked to bare their breasts and maybe more in public in exchange for beads. As this happens you can expect one or more other spectators to take still photos and videos. Girls who drink too much and engage in this behavior shouldn't be surprised to find that they have unwittingly become unpaid porn actresses.

This can also happen in bars and other venues where events like wet tee shirt contests also involve public exposure. They are often not limited to just topless displays. Body painting is also popular. This is where girls parade around the streets wearing only paint. Such events usually also involve binge drinking. As Orenstein points out, the so-called campus rape culture is centered around fraternity parties and usually involves women who drink to the point where their judgment is impaired or non-existent.

It's hard to tell how many young men approach their dates regarding BDSM (Bondage, Domination, Sadism, and Masochism), but some certainly do so. This can be dangerous for people who aren't trained in how to tie someone up without cutting off their circulation.

A trip to a local Adult store will convince you that this type of sexual activity has increased in popularity as the shelves will have all sorts of bondage gear along with floggers, whips, crops, and canes. I suspect that the popularity of the *50 Shades of Grey* series has had something to do with this. These stores use to sell a lot of DVDs, but now most of the shelf space is devoted to a wide variety of sex toys and apparel.

While women are usually on the receiving end of BDSM efforts, you can find videos where women work men over and where women are dishing it out to other women. If you are determined to give this a go, I suggest that you view some "how to" videos first. They are easy to find with simple Internet searches. For the literary crowd, there is no shortage of fiction dealing with every possible sexual niche. Many sites will even accept submissions from their readers.

Watching a lot of porn can have an impact on one's sex life. If you get to the point where you need this kind of stimulation to be aroused, real sex could be a problem. Ironically, boys who watch a lot of porn should have a much better idea of how to please a girl than pre-Internet males. Whether real or fake, most videos feature orgasms of some kind and how to get there.

The masturbation category is popular with boys, so they should know what a girl wants in the way of stimulation with one's fingers. Close-ups are common so boys should understand female anatomy and just where the clitoris is since they aren't likely to find it in sex ed class. In addition to the fellatio videos, there are also many that feature members of both genders giving oral sex to woman. They should provide pretty good how to videos for young men.

While girls watch less porn than boys, there are still many that do. Since there are so many lesbian videos featuring women who may or may not be lesbians, studies show that more girls are having sex with each other. From the girls' point of view, they are almost certain to receive pleasure, and pregnancy is out of the question. But beware, your boyfriend may ask to watch you have sex with another girl.

## Summary

In addition to having open conversations with their kids, parents should probably precede such conversations by getting at least a little hip about what is out there. Going to some of the popular sites and at least looking at the thumbnails on the home page and reading the names of the categories should be sufficient.

Unfortunately, there is a dearth of research on this topic. As you can imagine, institutions don't want to be associated with this subject and most professionals don't want to be seen as porn researchers. I doubt that I would even be writing this chapter were it not for the fact that I am happily retired and can't be fired. Research is also difficult to do, as some have noted, due to the fact that it is difficult to round up a control group of men who haven't seen Internet porn.

As I stated previously, if you find that your child has viewed some porn, use it as an opening for a conversation rather than an opportunity to administer negative consequences. To help you further understand online porn read Maureen O'Conner's article *Porn Is the Kinsey Report of Our Time.*

# References

Pornography Statistics 250+ facts, quotes, and statistics about pornography use, *Covenant Eyes*, (2015 Edition) http://bit.ly/29y52NE.

Dickson, EJ. Is Internet Porn Making Young Men Impotent? *Rolling Stone Online*, September 21, 2017, http://rol.st/2hnXwu3.

Gilkerson, Luke. Teens and Porn: 10 Stats You Need to Know, *Convenient Eyes*, August 19, 2010 http://bit.ly/1IkJSiz

O'Conor, Maureen. Pornhub Is the Kinsey Report of Our Time, *The Cut Online,* June 11, 2017, http://bit.ly/2rRQJiM.

Orenstein, Peggy (2016). *Girls and Sex: Navigating the Complicated New Landscape,* Harper Collins: New York, NY.

Zimmerman, Jonathan. *Too Hot To Handle: A Global History of Sex Education*, Princeton University Press: Princeton, NJ, 2015.

Wilson, Gary. The great porn experiment, TEDxGlasgow, May 16, 2012 http://bit.ly/2hjY7Rc.

# CHAPTER 20

# It's Time For An Assessment Revolution: Give Students Access To The Internet In Exams And Scrap Traditional Grades

"Students should commit some facts to memory to develop their critical thinking skills, but more tests need to reflect the real world." -Dr. Doug Green

IF A GOAL of education is to make students career-ready, why do we assess them in ways that have little or nothing to do with what people do on the job? If anyone at work realizes a need for information that they don't already know, be it isolated facts or how to do something, they probably won't wait too long before they look it up on the Internet.

In their book *Most Likely to Succeed: Preparing Our Kids for The Innovation ERA,* Tony Wagner and Ted Dintersmith argue that students should be able to use real-world tools as they take on any task or test that their teachers pose. They also point out that Denmark started doing this with some exams way back in 2009. I couldn't agree more.

With Internet search, facts are sitting ducks. Yet, many teachers base their student grades on tests that require lots of recall of facts and procedures without access to the tools students will use once they leave school. Also, in the real world, no one uses the math routines learned in school to do computations that can't be done quickly in their head. They simply fire up a spreadsheet program. In fact, if a supervisor caught an employee doing calculations by hand, a stern reprimand would likely follow.

As principal, I once caught the school secretary using a pocket calculator to add a list of numbers. To make things worse, it was the type of calculator that only showed one number at a time so she couldn't see if any numbers previously entered were entered in error. I told her that the device on her desk was called a computer in part because it was really good at computing. I then gave her lesson one on how to use a spreadsheet and told her I didn't want to see the pocket calculator in use as long as she was doing work for which she was being compensated. Don't worry; I also let her know that I still loved her.

My point with this story is that our assessment of students shouldn't focus on things they will *never* do when they hit the world of work. In my mind there is little reason to give tests that aren't open-Internet tests, just as in my day when teachers would occasionally give open book tests. My advanced organic chemistry final in grad school (Colgate University, 1970) was an open world test that allowed asking experts and it lasted a week. I think the professor was trying to get answers to questions related to his research that he didn't know. This sure makes sense.

## Another Benefit of Open-Internet Testing

Prior to the Internet, students were limited to information that they could find in libraries and other sources of published content. Most of the information available in a library is the product of experts in their fields. It has been selected by teaching and library staff in order to best meet the needs of students pursuing the pre-defined demands of the faculty.

Many of the resources were obtained to meet the needs of yesterday's faculty. As such, it is an extension of the accepted canon of knowledge that is dispensed by teachers in traditional classroom settings. It is the body of knowledge and opinion valued by teachers and their teachers for generations.

In contrast, the information available via the Internet also represents a rapidly expanding piece of the real world with all of its imperfections and diversity. The views and opinions of experts are joined by the more prosaic thoughts of anyone who cares to make a statement. Posting information for all to see is something that almost anyone can do.

This means that the voices of young and old, expert and novice, mainstream and marginal, conservative and liberal, radical and reactionary, gay and straight, rich and homeless, X and Y (Feel free to fill in your own set of opposites) all contribute to the dynamic daily debate on any subject one can imagine.

This means that students using the Internet as a tool for completing assignments and assessments need to evaluate the quality of the information they find. This requires the kind of critical thinking and problem solving that most educators promote and that all businesses want. It also means that teachers will have to provide lessons on techniques for vetting what students find.

## Students Should Memorize Some Facts

I'm not saying that students shouldn't commit some facts and procedures to long-term memory. I also think there is a place for working on the recall of the basic facts, concepts, and principles associated with the disciplines at hand.

As Benedict Carey points out in *How We Learn: The Surprising Truth About When, Where, and Why It Happens,* working on recalling what you are trying to learn is more effective than additional efforts to memorize it. Self-testing then is far more important than more study.

Even though you can look up just about anything, your long-term memory is vital to any kind of critical thinking and problem solving.

The reason for having knowledge in long-term memory is that when you try to solve a problem, all you have access to is long-term memory and information from your current environment. Therefore, the more you have in long-term memory, the more tools you have for solving any given problem. Having to look everything up, however, would be inefficient to the point where little would get done.

As students encounter information in multiple real-world contexts, they will internalize important items. Self-testing can be facilitated by computer-based question banks. Mastered content reported to teachers will allow them to help students decide what to work on next.

When it comes to assessing student competence, there is a serious trend that I agree with using real-world, open-ended projects that allow for unlimited use of any tools students can get their hands on, such as Internet search and spreadsheets. You can even get the Internet to do calculus homework with Wolfram Alpha. I haven't used calculus in decades but I'm sure I could pass just about any calc test using this resource.

## Grab A Larger Audience For Student Work

The results of student efforts should also be made available to a larger audience. Many teachers are starting to publish student work on class blogs for the world to see. Some also require students to view and comment on each other's work, and some students have their own blogs. It is also vital that students evaluate their own work. This thinking about one's thinking is called metacognition and is widely considered a powerful aid to effective learning.

If you think that getting rid of traditional grades based largely on fact-based closed Internet tests will be a problem when it comes to college acceptance, think again. Colleges already require and evaluate portfolios for art students and home-schooled students. In my daughter's case, her art portfolio contained her best work from all four years of her high school career and its quality was the biggest factor in college acceptance.

Portfolios of student work would also let employers see what a student is capable of doing and some employers now require it. This beats a list of courses and grades as far as I'm concerned. It also demonstrates a connection with the real world that regurgitated facts and procedures and the grades they generate cannot. Artists who are looking for work, for example, put together what they call a reel. This is a two-minute video that contains samples of their best work. Once they know what a specific employer is looking for, they are likely to modify their reel accordingly. (Here is the link to my daughter's reel. http://bit.ly/2ACjHbV)

Some schools have begun the process of switching from grades to badges. As you may know, this is how scouting organizations allow members to show competence. Such badges are often part of a flipped/mastery teaching system that I discuss in a later chapter. This is where students view direct instruction at their own pace on a laptop and spend class time getting help from the teacher, working alone or with other students, or taking online unit tests when they think they are ready. For more details on this topic, see *Flip Your Classroom: Reach Every Student in Every Classroom Every Day* by Jonathan Bergman and Arron Sams. You can start by reading my summary. http://bit.ly/1atBiOe.

## Bringing The Real World Into Lessons Is A Hot Idea

It is easy to find authors in the world of education talk about the importance of connecting the real world with the curriculum. While the classroom is somewhat separate from the rest of the real world, the Internet can take students to a much more in-your-face version of the real real-world.

Teachers need to be ready for how this will change their practice. As students search the Internet for assignments and assessments, they will no doubt find information with which the teacher isn't familiar. This means that the teachers no longer own the information. This will complicate grading as well, which is one more reason why we should give up on traditional grades.

Student use of the Internet for assessments will no doubt produce reports and projects regarding which teachers will need to review and offer feedback to students. The best way to get better at anything is to do it a lot while getting feedback from someone with expertise in that field. By shifting direct instruction to Internet videos, teachers should find that they have more time for giving students valuable feedback. Feedback that is much more useful than grades. If you must give a grade, never give it at the same time you give your feedback if you want your students to even read the feedback.

# References

Adams Becker, S., Freeman, A., Giesinger Hall, C., Cummins, M., and Yuhnke, B. (2016). NMC/CoSN Horizon Report: 2016 K-12 Edition. Austin, Texas: *The New Media Consortium, http://bit.ly/2suespE.*

Bergmann, Jonathan and Sams, Arron (2012). *Flip Your Classroom: Reach Every Student in Every Classroom Every Day,* International Society for Technology in Education: Washington, DC.

Carey, Benedict. *How We Learn: The Surprising Truth About When, Where, and Why It Happens* by Benedict Carey, Random House: New York, NY, 2014.

Michaelsen, Ann. Connected Test-Taking: Is It Cheating? Powerful Learning Practice Blog, May 3, 2012, http://bit.ly/2eC8hbB

Wagner, Tony and Dintersmith, Ted. *Most Likely to Succeed: Preparing Our Kids for The Innovation Era.* Scribner: New York, NY, 2015.

# CHAPTER 21

# Why Would Anyone Let Their Kid Play Football or Anything Else?

"Football is the New Smoking." -Dr. Doug Green

"I'm seeing these overuse injuries in younger and younger people." -Michael A. Kelly, MD, chairman of the Department of Orthopedic Surgery at the Hackensack University Medical Center

WHEN I WAS growing up in the 1950s, my parents smoked a great deal. My father even smoked in the car. This was before cigarette packs had draconian warnings on the side, which today pretty much say: "smoke and you die." Google "cigarette warning labels" if you want to see some of the really scary ones from other countries.

Back then it was obvious to me and many others that smoking was unhealthy. At the time, many smokers were in denial as some are today, but the jury has certainly spoken about the risks you take if you smoke or even breathe someone else's smoke.

When I reached high school in the 1960s, football was the glamour sport, as it still is in many schools. Fortunately for myself, I didn't have the physical attributes to participate at the varsity level. As a result, I have spent my life concussion-free and even though I recently turned seventy, my brain and body work just fine and all of my joints are original equipment.

Up until recently, I hadn't given much thought about how football might be bad for the brain. Within the last few years, however, we have seen many news stories suggesting a connection between playing football and subsequent trips to the dementia spectrum.

The movie *Concussion* has also brought the dangers of playing football to the public's attention. Set in 2002, the film stars Will Smith as Dr. Bennet Omalu, a forensic pathologist who fights against the National Football League, which is trying to suppress his research on chronic traumatic encephalopathy (CTE), brain degeneration suffered by professional football players.

It doesn't seem possible that most of our population failed to connect the act of repeated collisions with brain damage. Once you realize that boxing for a living had something to do with Muhammad Ali's deteriorated mental condition, it's not a big stretch to believe that football could have a similar effect.

We may have reached a tipping point as 57 percent of parents, according to a recent ESPN survey, say that the recent news makes them concerned about letting their kids play youth football. It seems, therefore, that it is just a matter of time before schools either fail to field a team or cancel football to avoid liability issues. Two school districts near where I live have merged their football teams due to lack of participation.

## Violence as a Spectator Sport

You might wonder how it is that we ever thought that a sport where the central idea was to run as fast as you can and collide with other people was a good idea. It's no secret that people in general love to watch violence. Where would the gladiators have been without this essential human emotion?

Watching people who don't know better beat the crap out of

each other might be fun for some, but how about when it's your own flesh and blood? While violent movies and computer games are very popular, most of our population limits violence viewing to the virtual variety, with the exception of football.

So let's assume that it won't be long before almost all parents take a pass on letting their kids play football as we know it. The question then becomes, what should parents let their kids do? Flashing back to my youth again, I recall that after school or on non-school days, my mother usually told me to go out and play and to be home in time for dinner.

My geographical limits were those imposed by my bicycle skills, and it wasn't unusual for me to roam the neighborhood armed with a BB gun and/or a bow with metal-tipped arrows. I played in a nearby swamp and garbage dump. This was before wetlands and landfills were invented. In modern terms I was a free-range child. I played pick-up baseball, basketball, and touch football along with other classic childhood games and games we made up. Based on people I have talked to in my generation, my experience was fairly common.

Today if a parent lets their kids roam the neighborhood unsupervised they run the risk of being turned in for neglect and some have been. Parents with means enroll their kids in various sporting activities, which almost always require driving the kids to the location of the activity and hanging out on the sidelines. As Amanda Ripely points out in her book "The Smartest Kids in the World," the kids would be farther ahead academically if the parents spent this time reading with the kids and discussing what they read.

As for safety, kids are at greater risk of injury due to an automobile accident than if they were simply roaming the neighborhood unsupervised. Check these quotes from Kristen Jensen's article *The epidemic that's ruining youth sports* in the June 20, 2017 *New York Post*.

> A 2015 survey in the American Journal of Sports Medicine found that 60 percent of all Tommy John surgeries in the U.S. are for patients aged 15 to 19.

The largest cause of many injuries is young athletes specializing in one sport at an earlier age. Instead of playing lacrosse, basketball and football, they are opting to stick with just one, and it's taking a toll on their bodies.

We're seeing re-injuries more commonly in the last ten years. And these are injuries that are not reversible. By the time these kids move into the next generation, we're going to be seeing [joint] replacements at a younger and younger age.

## Football Isn't the Only Risk

Although football is probably the number one culprit, a quick look at available data shows that concussions and other injuries aren't limited to football. Just about any sport that schools run offers opportunities for life-changing injuries, but some are certainly safer than others. Parents should certainly beware of contact sports such as basketball, soccer, and lacrosse.

Sports with projectiles like baseball, softball, and lacrosse offer additional opportunities for injury. Once you get past concussions, the next most popular injuries with serious consequences seem to be tears or breaks of the ligaments surrounding the knee.

Then there are the sports where overuse comes into play. Too much running or throwing can cause injuries to arms and legs. While running seems like a good thing to do, too much can be a problem. Perhaps the biggest risk for girls is cheerleading. When I was in high school, the cheerleaders barely got off the floor, and no one I know remembers a cheerleader injury from my era.

Today, some cheerleading teams don't even cheer at games as they are focused on preparing for cheerleading competitions. If you haven't seen one of these affairs, you should give it a try. They feature girls standing on each other, throwing each other about, manic tumbling, and all sorts of opportunities for serious injuries. I have yet to attend a large-scale competition that didn't feature at least one girl, usually more, being taken out in a wheel chair or on a stretcher. If your kid plays a sport that features an EMT van on the sideline, you should probably think again.

The overuse problem is being exacerbated by students who are pressured to play the same sport all year long. Coaches who only care about their sport are at fault, as are parents who think they are raising kids to win college scholarships. Once the season ends for a school sport, there are options for so-called travel and AAU team play as long as parents can make it possible. Once again poor kids are at a disadvantage although they might suffer fewer serious injuries.

Schools seldom offer dance or martial arts, but they are usually available in most communities. Ironically martial arts programs are very low in injury frequency as is dance, at least for starters. More advanced ballet can feature lifts and dancing on one's toes for which the toe is poorly designed. If you ever get a look at an adult ballerina's feet, you will know what I mean.

## Paying For Other Kids' Play

Another problem with school sports is that every high school has one of each kind of team they can support, no matter the school's size. My high school was so big that a very small percentage of the students could play anything. In spite of the fact that I couldn't make a team, my parents still paid taxes that supported all the teams.

This is why other countries run sports through clubs that are not associated with schools. In these systems the people who play are the people who pay, along with team sponsors. At the other end of the spectrum are small schools where just about every able-bodied student has to play just to field a team, and almost every student plays three sports.

## Academic Injuries

As for academics, school sports programs are a clear cause of poorer performance than might otherwise be the case. Students who are serious about sports certainly have less time for any kind of serious study. Ironically, athletes often out perform non athletes due mostly to the fact that they have more discipline and a better work ethic.

At the college level we have seen situations where students take courses that don't exist and still get passing grades, and where team managers write the papers. Even when so-called student athletes take a course, they are usually off the easy course, easy professor list that you can find in any frat house or athletic department.

The fact that schools run extensive athletic programs also impacts hiring practices. In many cases when principals are hiring, the person who can teach and coach will get the nod over one that can only teach, regardless of teaching skill. This has to have the effect of reducing the overall quality of the teaching staff to some extent.

For many coaches, their real passion is the sport they coach rather than the classes they teach. The time they spend planning, running practices, traveling, and coaching games must result in less effort associated with creating great classroom activities. It probably also has a negative impact on their family life, and coaches are more likely to be involved in questionable activities with students than many other educator types.

## What Should a Caring Parent Do?

With many schools cutting back on recess to focus on test prep, parents should pay attention to keeping their kids active. Exercising with your kids seems like the best idea. This allows parents and children to stay fit together and sets a great example for children. Even just walking can promote health and give parents and their children time to talk.

As for school programs, cross country is probably one of the safest and best in terms of fitness as long as you don't run too many miles. Unlike sports such as basketball where teams usually consist of about twelve players and only five play at a time, there is no reason for the cross country coach to cut anyone, no matter how slow he or she is. The same should be true for the track team, which in some schools feature winter and spring programs.

Other sports that seem safer and shouldn't limit participation are swimming, golf, tennis, and bowling. I played on the golf team in high school. While I wasn't good enough to play in any competitions, I was able to play for free every day after school in the spring. I walked and carried my bag on a hilly course, so I know it helped with my fitness.

While most school employees look down on home-schooling, kids that are home-schooled can have a much more robust and healthy exercise program. I am familiar with some situations in which the kids take breaks with other home-schooled kids mid-morning and mid-afternoon for exercise activities. Such activities can serve to fill the socialization gap caused by not going to school. These kids can also stand and walk about any time and don't need a hall pass to go to the bathroom. Where I live they meet at the local YMCA and Boys and Girls Club for swimming or other kinds of exercise.

Schools and individual teachers can address this. I have seen elementary teachers who get their kids out of their seats on a regular basis for calisthenics or at least a walk around the halls. Some secondary schools build in longer gaps between two periods in the morning and afternoon so that students can walk or run. I visited one inner city high school without a gym where there was organized running in the hallway twice a day.

## Think Long Term

Thanks to my limited skills, I not only missed playing football, I also missed out on life-altering injuries. I have a number of friends my age who made the team at their schools who are now less fit and less able to engage in exercise due to bad backs and artificial joints. I'm sure that it won't be too long before one or more hits the dementia spectrum.

It should be clear to parents that kids need to move on a regular basis, but if that movement involves charging into other people, it's not a good idea. So when it's time to sign your kid up for youth football, *just say no!* Your child might not like it if his friends are playing, so be ready for a battle. This is a battle that is worth winning.

# References

Fleming, Kirsten. The epidemic that's ruining youth sports, *The New York Post,* June 20. 2017, http://nyp.st/2rQtceI.

Powell, Michale. North Carolina's Dominance Fails to Cover Cheating's Stain, *New York Times*, March 31, 2017 http://nyti.ms/2rpFFZL.

Ripley, Amanda (2013). *The Smartest Kids in the World and How They Got That Way*, Simon and Schuster: New York, NY.

# CHAPTER 22

# Bathrooms and Locker Rooms: A New Battlefield

"What we need is more privacy for all students rather than worrying about who uses which bathroom and which locker room." -Dr. Doug Green

AUTHOR'S NOTE: THIS is a complicated topic that our society is currently grappling with. While I do offer a way to deal with the situation, this chapter asks a lot more questions than it answers.

It's hard to imagine you haven't heard about the controversy at a Palatine, Illinois high school, where a transgender girl playing on a girls' sports team is demanding unfettered access to the girls' locker room. Along these same lines the city of Houston, Texas recently voted no on a proposition that, among other things, would let anyone use any bathroom based on the gender with which they identify.

Now that schools are facing these issues I hope we can come up with solutions that can work for people on both sides of this matter and not create a lot of distractions. For one, I find it easy to sympathize with transgender students as I'm sure that they face a difficult and in some cases hostile world, where some oppose their personal choices.

The person in question in Palatine was born a male and later started to identify as a female. This included taking on a girl's name, dressing as a girl, and expecting the school to treat "her" accordingly. One problem some people have here is that she still has male parts. No doubt the parents of some girls are concerned about the possibility that their daughter will be exposed to male private parts in a school locker room.

What is more curious to me, though, is why the school was quick to allow this child to play on the girls' team. Suppose your daughter was the last girl cut on a team that featured one or more positions occupied by girls with male bodies? Does this change the dynamic of the game being played? For contact sports would girls be at a greater risk when competing with opponents born as males? (See a previous chapter regarding sports safety in general.)

How would other schools in their league and the league itself handle this? Should one school have an advantage on the field because a team contains players who are physically boys? Since boys on average are bigger and stronger than girls, does this seem fair? At the national, international, and Olympic levels, women have to prove that they are indeed females in order to participate in women's events. Why should this be any different at the high school level?

## Girls On the Boy's Team

High school girls have occasionally played on boys teams, and their generally smaller bodies don't give the team an unfair advantage. This happens in sports like golf where schools don't have a girls' team. I've seen it in football where the girl on the team is most likely the place kicker. Girls on wrestling teams are not uncommon. In this case size isn't an issue due to weight divisions. I've also seen girls on baseball and bowling teams, but I haven't heard of any outcry about locker rooms as a result. This is because girls on boys' teams simply use the girls' locker room.

Some people in Houston say they voted against men in women's bathrooms even though the proposal in question was much broader than that. Some also expressed a worry that cross-dressing men could engage in inappropriate behavior if allowed. Schools, however, can better control their bathrooms and privacy shouldn't be an issue if all one finds in locker rooms and bathrooms are private lockable stalls. It's not like the boy's room where the use of urinals are somewhat less private. Schools that allow anyone to use any bathroom are certainly more likely to get complaints from girls and their parents even though privacy should be less of an issue in girl's bathrooms as they only contain individual stalls.

In an ideal world, all bathrooms would be unisex, and that seems to be the trend. For schools this would add to the cost, so many schools let transgender kids use single stall rooms that are often designed for staff. Unfortunately, this isn't good enough for some students, parents, and organizations that support LGBT issues. This seems to sort itself out as a liberal/conservative issue with the liberal outlets like the "New York Times" editorial page being all for total transgender rights.

As for locker rooms in schools, it's rare today for students to shower after physical education classes. This issue is more about athletic teams where players may take showers after workouts and games. There are other venues, however, where modesty is not a big deal. If a transgender boy decided to use the locker room at the YMCA I attend for example, he would get quite a show regarding male anatomy. Ideally, locker rooms would be set up where every player has a stall for changing and showering in private. This would be expensive, but it would help in a number of ways.

In addition to the transgender issue, there is the matter of gay students in locker rooms, and supervising adults seeing naked young student bodies. I fully support gay rights, but I suspect that some straight people would rather not have to undress in front of someone of their gender physically attracted to people of their gender. While private showers won't solve every problem, they do offer all students a degree of privacy that they deserve. For now the free alternative is for kids to throw on a sweat suit and shower at home. This also gets rid of shower supervision issues and the school saves on hot water.

As a retired principal, I'm from an age when I swam naked in the YMCA pool as a kid. I've also been to beaches in Europe where people were mostly or totally nude. Since I was a child, our culture has changed and students are far more modest. I see this as a good thing, and I encourage leaders on both sides of the argument to focus on the privacy in all aspects of the issue rather than putting children into situations where they could be exposed to bodies of students born with a different gender. I think we can have equal treatment for all if we work together and keep this issue from becoming another political football. It would also allow schools to focus on doing a better job facilitating student learning.

## References

Berman, Russell. How Bathroom Fears Conquered Transgender Rights in Houston, *The Atlantic,* November 3, 2016, http://theatln. tc/2rZ6vFs.

Eldeib, Duaa. Transgender student rights: Education Department, courts not on same page, *The Chicago Tribune,* November 3, 2015, http://trib.in/2rZg2ML.

National School Boards Association. Christian advocacy group calling on New York state district to reverse policy allowing a transgender student to use the boys' restroom and locker room facilities, *Legal Clips: National School Boards Association* November 6, 201,5 http:// bit.ly/1WDyurV.

New York Times Editorial Board. Support Houston's Equal Rights Ordinance, *The New York Times,* November 2, 2015, http://nyti. ms/2rq0q7S.

The Alliance for Gay, Lesbian, Bisexual, Transgender and Questioning Youth. The Alliance was developed in response to findings from our community needs assessment to address the absence of comprehensive and coordinated services for GLBTQ youth in Miami-Dade County, Florida. Visit their homepage http://bit.ly/2rZpsYr.

CHAPTER **23**

# How Do We Know That Today's Standardized Tests Are Harmful?

"These tests are designed to sort kids more than to find out what they know. Would you want to be sorted?" -Dr. Doug Green

TO ANSWER THIS question, I direct you to two books. The first is *The Myths of Standardized Testing: Why They Don't Tell You What You Think They Do* by Phillip Harris, Bruce M. Smith, and Joan Harris (with a little help from ten of their friends.) I suggest you start with my summary here http://bit.ly/1Nunc0C. The authors believe that our schools are under attack by the tests that continue to seep into our schools. They sap the energy and enthusiasm of educators and drain the life from children's learning.

Standardized tests depend on the idea that a small portion of a student's behavior fairly represents the whole range of possible behavior. To draw valid inferences from a test, it must cover more than a small part of the content domain. If you have a large number of students, overall outcomes on different versions of a test should even out. But any one student can go from proficient on one version to needing remediation on another.

Items are chosen to spread out the scores of the test-takers. The best items discriminate between students at various levels of achievement. For example, you would want an item that every student would answer correctly except the very lowest performers. Other items would discriminate at various ability levels all the way to the top. The idea is to sort kids by ability. I, for one, don't think that schools should be in the business of sorting kids. Time limits spread out scores even more, as some students can't finish.

## The Tests Aren't Objective

By *objective* adherents of this idea mean: based on observable phenomena and not influenced by emotion or personal prejudice. A look at how the tests are made, however, reveals a good deal of subjective human judgment from the people who write, edit, and assemble the test items. Setting the standards also requires judgment that occurs in a political and social context.

Achievement levels are, first and foremost, policy statements. The only truly objective part is the scoring. Test scores are not clean, crisp numbers but fuzzy ranges that extend above and below the score, and 5% of the time the true score isn't even in the fuzzy error range. Since numbers confer a sense of fairness and impartiality, they are used to justify decisions that impact students' lives.

Campbell's law states: "The more any quantitative social indicator is used for social decision-making, the more it will be subject to corruption pressures, and the more apt it will be to distort and corrupt the social processes it was intended to monitor." So if the stakes are high, people will work harder to improve. Such hard work can subvert the accuracy of the measurement. If test preparation is excessive, the tested students will no longer compare to the group on which the test was normed.

Schools caught cheating constitute only the tip of the iceberg. Some schools improve scores by counseling students to drop out into GED programs. Educational triage takes place when teachers focus on "bubble kids" who will pass with help at the expense of others, like top kids, who will pass no matter what the teacher does or low kids who stand no chance of passing. Lots of test prep also takes time from non-tested subjects. (See my earlier chapter on cheating.)

## Students as Stuffed Turkeys

Although most educators think depth is more important than breadth of coverage, the proliferation of state-level standards results in the polar opposite. Teachers survey entire fields to "cover" the curriculum and stuff kids like turkeys with as many facts as possible. The impact is even starker in areas that are not tested.

High-stakes tests have narrowed and dumbed down curricula and eliminated time spent on untested subjects by about a third, including recess. The fact that this happened was not part of discussions that lead to the tests in the first place. Tests also drive instruction toward items with one clear, right answer at the expense of open-ended problem solving and projects. Explaining is hard to do when you are blackening a bubble and collaboration is seen as cheating. Ironically, the people pushing the tests also want to hire people skilled at collaboration.

The authors cite a 2008 work by Richard Rothstein, which proposes that assessment efforts need to be more broad. He lists the categories that should be judged: basic knowledge and skills, critical thinking and problem solving, social skills and work ethic, citizenship and community responsibility, appreciation of arts and literature, preparation for skilled work, physical health, and emotional health.

## Rethinking Value-Added Models in Education

The second book to consider is *Rethinking Value-Added Models in Education: Critical Perspective on Tests and Assessment-Based Accountability* by Audrey Amrein-Beardsley. See my summary here: http://bit.ly/1zaiI6Y. It describes and analyzes the imposition of value added test-based evaluation of teachers, the theory behind it, the real-life consequences, and its fundamental flaws.

VAMs as they are called, are statistical tools used to measure the purportedly causal relationships between having been instructed by teacher A and achieving a specific growth over a certain time while controlling for various student background characteristics. Gains are measured between current and previous scores, which allows students to act as their own controls.

If VAMs are used in your state, check to see which student factors are controlled for such as race, ethnicity, poverty, and English proficiency. VAMs have a norm referenced feel as by definition about 50% of teachers are typically categorized as adding value and the other 50% are categorized as subtracting it. Whenever you see percentiles used, as they are in New York, it's a zero sum game. For every student that moves up one or more percentiles, another student has to go down. This means that for every teacher who appears to add value, another appears to subtract value.

Audrey makes a compelling case here that VAMs are unreliable, invalid, biased, unfair, and fraught with measurement errors. They are therefore used inappropriately to make consequential decisions while unintended consequences go unrecognized. Meanwhile, private companies sell their VAM models to schools for profit.

## We Don't Randomly Assign Students

Students are not randomly assigned to classes and teachers feel that the scores their students achieve are largely due to the nature of the students they teach. It is also common for teachers to score high one year and low the next even though they aren't doing anything different. This is known as regression to the mean, which is important to understand here. VAM scores also lack transparency, as teachers by and large don't have any idea about how they work.

The author's experience shows that 95% of educational researchers protest the use of any of the available models. Unfortunately, forty-four states and D.C. as of this writing (2014) use some form of VAM to evaluate teachers. In all cases, empirical evidence shows that the models have serious questions regarding reliability, validity, and bias, and should therefore not be used in any high-stakes decision-making process.

If these scores were reliable, you would expect experienced teachers to get the same or nearly the same scores each year. Year to year correlations of VAM scores for individual teachers are low enough in most cases that you can see how little the individual teacher impacts the scores. Students who take more than one version of a test also show wide variations in scores. Thus the scores are not reliable and are therefore invalid.

## Who Thought Test and Punish Was a Good Idea

Many teachers are rewarded or punished based on where they teach and who they teach as opposed to how well they teach. Teachers of poor, ELL, and special education students fall into this category. Gifted teachers can also have a difficult time showing growth since their high-scoring students cannot improve test scores that are already at or near the top of the distribution.

Another problem is related to student mobility and the law of small numbers. For a teacher with a class of twenty students, the class size isn't large enough to produce statistically significant results. No researcher worth his or her salt would dream of using such a small sample. This is compounded by the fact that almost all teachers will experience some level of student mobility during the school year.

In New York, the only students who count for a school or a teacher are those enrolled by the first Monday in October and who stay continuously until the tests are given in April and May. At the school where I taught, we had an annual mobility rate of around 37% each year. This means that for most teachers the number of students who counted for their evaluation was closer to thirteen.

While this book is written for an academic audience, it is one that should be on the shelf of every school's professional development library. We can also hope that it gets into the hands of as many policy makers as possible. See what you can do to make that happen and do what you can do to fight the insanity forced on our children by the corporate/political class that demands objective numbers in a field that does not lend itself to strictly objective evaluation.

# References

Amrein-Beardsley, Audrey. *Rethinking Value-Added Models in Education: Critical Perspective on Tests and Assessment-Based Accountability*, 2014: Routledge, New York, NY.

Harris, Phillip, Smith, Bruce M, and Harris Joan. *The Myths of Standardized Testing: Why They Don't Tell You What You Think They Do*, 2011, Rowman and Littlefield Publishers: Lanham, MD.

# If Education Is Going To Improve, We Must Work On Improving Initial Teacher Training

"Increased teacher contact time and observations are just two of the many strategies we should try to adopt from Finland's model for preparing new teachers." -Dr. Doug Green

WE ARE ALL concerned with improving the education our students receive. But instead of focusing on the classroom, we need to take a step back. If education is going to improve, we must work on improving initial teacher training.

I said in a previous chapter that education isn't rocket science, it's much more complicated, and our system for preparing new teachers is not making life any simpler or more effective. In the U.S. alone there are 1,500 institutions that train teachers, and approaches vary a great deal depending on state regulations and the leaders' vision.

There are two aspects to this process. The coursework generally covers content, methods, and psychology. Newer courses also deal with technology integration and issues related to culture and diversity.

The other aspect places students in schools for observations and student teaching. Many colleges have students visit schools to observe veteran teachers in action prior to their senior year. As seniors, students are placed with a cooperating teacher for a period that averages about ten weeks.

Students start by observing and assisting the cooperating teacher; then at some point they take over planning and delivering lessons. How long they get to do this varies, depending on what the cooperating teacher decides and what the college requires.

## A Solo Week?

As an elementary principal, I was shocked to learn that most student teachers had only one "solo week" during which they did everything with the cooperating teacher often out of the room. This isn't enough. Some colleges require two student teaching placements in different schools and one placement needs to have a special education focus. This is better but still insufficient.

In Finland, students spend an entire year of apprenticeship in a school working with multiple teachers, and are required to complete a research-based masters degree prior to beginning their teaching career.

Finland is also much more selective when it comes to admitting students into teacher training programs. In the U.S., these programs are often not very selective. As a result, we graduate many more teachers than we need in disciplines like elementary education and not enough in other disciplines like science, technology, and special education.

The task of preparing teachers is complicated further by the Common Core Standards and the associated standardized testing. There is also the matter of the many innovative teaching strategies being rolled out in some schools and classrooms that are not included in many college programs. Such innovations include flipping learning, project-based learning, extensive student collaboration, student internships, blended learning, and one-to-one programs where every student has a laptop.

Another key issue is the selection of cooperating teachers. Colleges often require that they are experienced, effective, and possess strong mentoring skills. This severely limits the pool of possible participants. The K-12 schools have a great deal of control here. In my case, for example, I let the colleges know which of my teachers were available to take a student teacher.

The fact that teachers are often evaluated in part by student test scores limits the pool further. Who wants to turn their class over to a rookie when they will be judged on their students' performance? This is just one more negative consequence that results from the standardized testing madness. Schools also get pushback from parents who don't want their kids taught by student teachers.

## We Should Try To Adopt As Much Of Finland's Model As Possible.

While teachers in training need to familiarize themselves with the Common Core standards and the associated tests, it is also vital that they observe and participate with cooperating teachers using as many innovative methods as possible for as long as possible. Such observations can even start while future teachers are in high school.

For each class they visit they should be assigned one or more students to get to know. The students selected for such mentoring should include the neediest students who may have disruptive tendencies. Some observations should also take place on the first day of school as many student teachers never see day one until they get their first teaching job.

Teacher candidates should visit classes where group projects are in action so they can facilitate small group activity. It also makes sense to work with small groups prior to dealing with an entire class.

The most important part of new teacher training should focus on how teachers can build strong working relationships with their students. The research I do daily is convincing me that there is an emerging consensus on the primary importance of relationships. As I noted in the previous chapter, consistently treating *all* students with respect is perhaps the best way to jump start strong relationships.

Extensive observations with multiple teachers in more than one school should expose student teachers to a variety of approaches for managing classrooms and redirecting undesirable behavior. This is where relationships make all the difference. I would also expose them to a variety of demographics.

## Don't Let Your Ego Get In the Way

It's important to see veteran teachers who don't let their egos get in the way. If you see lots of teachers in action, you can also learn from some who may be negative examples. Listening to a teacher use sarcasm, yell, and/or denigrate students in front of an entire class should convince a budding teacher that such behavior just doesn't work. Even low performing students can spot disdain when they see it.

If standardized testing is scaled back or ultimately eliminated, young teachers need to be ready to teach in ways they were probably never taught by their college professors. The same is true for professors preparing new teachers. Some have yet to see things like flipped classrooms or classes where every student has a laptop. This implies that university education departments should be more hands on when it comes to the professional development of their teaching staff. From what I have seen, professors are on their own when it comes to keeping up with innovative teaching trends.

New methods reveal a need to retrofit the teaching practices of at least some, if not most, of the professor class. For the most part, we are dealing with people who left the classroom long ago and some have little or no direct K-12 teaching experience. Many still mostly lecture when they lead courses for new teachers; they need to model the kind of innovative teaching they expect to see instead.

Trainees and their professors alike need to be ready for innovations such as badges in place of grades, schools without grade levels, self-paced personalized learning, real-world, long-term projects, and efforts to create self-directed learners. There is also an increased emphasis on allowing students to pursue their own interests and passions and to evaluate their own work.

# References

Amrein-Beardsley, A and Geiger, T. All Sizzle and No Steak: Value-Added Model Doesn't Add Value in Houston, *Phi Delta Kappan*, October 2017.

Bergmann, Jonathan and Sams, Arron (2012). *Flip Your Classroom: Reach Every Student in Every Classroom Every Day,* International Society for Technology in Education: Washington, DC.

Green, Douglas. Teaching Isn't Rocket Science, It's Way More Complex, *tes School News International Magazine,* August 31, 2016, http://bit.ly/2bIXvMU.

Hepburn, Henry. How to improve schools from start to Finnish, *tes School News International Magazine*, September 16, 2016, http://bit.ly/2rtdJ7v.

Sahlberg, Pasi (2015). *Finnish Lessons 2.0*: *What Can the World Can Learn From Educational Change in Finland*, Teachers College Press: New York, NY.

Ward, Helen. Schools don't seem able to give up levels, leaked report finds, *tes School News International Magazine*, July 28, 2015, http://bit.ly/2rt1MP4.

Wright, Sara. The 30-second briefing: What is flipped learning? *tes School News International Magazine,* July 13, 2016, http://bit.ly/2rtqcbh.

# CHAPTER 25

# Five Ways Hectically Busy School Leaders Can Stay on Track

"Trying to run a school can feel like a game of Whack-a-Mole, but there are ways to keep winning." -Dr. Doug Green

AS A PRINCIPAL I was fond of saying, "If you don't have ADHD when you take the job, you will have it two weeks later." I supervised 70 adults and dealt with 530 students and their parents, as well as my fellow administrators and the Superintendent. It only took a small subset of this horde wanting my attention at the same time for the job to begin to seem like playing the 'Whack-a-Mole' carnival game.

Anyone who aspires to this job needs to realize this and be prepared to deal with it. As a principal for thirteen years, (and an administrator for thirty years) I believe I managed the hectic pace with success, so for anyone who wants this job or who already has it, here are my top tips on how to stay on track.

## 1. Work Out What Can Wait

The ability to prioritize in a nimble manner is vital. This is a skill that can be improved with practice. When I taught leadership courses for teachers who sought principal certificates, I did just that. I gave them 'Whack a Mole' situations where multiple things were happening at the same time.

I asked them to figure out what to do on their own and then put them in groups to compare answers, come to a consensus, and share with the class. I also shared what I would do. I used real examples from my practice and had them harvest the same from their building principals and superintendents for further practice.

Here is an example. A teacher is upset that a vehicle is in her parking spot. An angry parent is in the office and wants to see you immediately. The breakfast line has stopped as two food service staff are arguing. You have a meeting with the superintendent in ten minutes. What do you do?* (Answer below)

## 2. All You Need Is Love

View the students and staff you serve as if they are all God's children. I think this is a good outlook even if you aren't so sure about God. You don't get paid to viscerally dislike anyone. It also amounts to self-imposed stress.

You don't have to accept behavior you find inappropriate, but as you deal with it, the people involved should feel that you still care about them. This may not seem directly related to 'Whack a Mole' problems, but if you act this way, people will cut you more slack and be more likely to pitch in to help. It's all about relationship building which, as I discussed in a previous chapter, is the most important thing that educators do.

## 3. Diet and Exercise

To get a lot done you need to be fit. Busy administrators tend to get bogged down in daily activities and promise themselves that they will make time later for exercise. The easiest way to build a fit foundation is to be visible. It's known as management by wandering around. It wasn't unusual for me to log forty plus miles a week as a principal, which included thousands of stairs in my four-story school.

Being visible will allow you to address things as people who see you can grab your ear. It will make them more efficient since they won't have to wait in line outside your office to see you. It will also give you more time to foster relationships with students and staff. You don't have to be thin to be fit, but fight the urge to snack whenever you find food in your path (unlike many administrators I know).

As an active principal, I put in so many miles and stairs during the week, I often used the weekend to recover. It is possible to exercise too much so try not to go overboard. A step counter on your cell phone can help you see at a glance when you have been moving too little or if you need some rest. I also do a thirty-minute weight routine twice a week so that all of my major muscle groups stay fit. I complement this with some time on my bicycle, walking while I play golf, and cross country skiing in the winter.

Ideally, you can turn exercise into a healthy addiction. Not only will this help you control stress, it will allow you to be a positive role model for students and staff. Don't hesitate to ask potential employees about their exercise plan. If you hire fit people they will also serve as student role models.

## You Are What You Eat

As for diet, the current research indicates that you should do two things. First, stop eating foods full of refined sugar and don't add sugar to the food you eat. Sorry folks, that means you should give up sugary drinks and as much dessert as possible. I no longer eat dessert at home where I eat most of my meals. I do politely eat desserts offered at friends' houses, but that's about it. Here I refer you to Gary Taubes' fine book *The Case Against Sugar*. In it he compares sugar to tobacco as both industries did what they could to promote their products while hiding the negative effects.

The second thing to do is to make vegetables the focus of your diet. They contain the variety of vitamins and minerals that your body needs, along with abundant fiber. Many, such as beans and peas, are also rich in protein. Be sure to avoid added salt and use a variety of other spices to make your food tasty.

In my case, I often use tasty meats like bacon and sausage in small quantities to spice up my vegetable dishes. I do the same with eggs and cheese. I will also have an occasional meal of chicken and fish. Like my consumption of desserts, I will eat other meat dishes at friends' houses.

If you eat bread make sure it is whole grain. If you are concerned about wheat products due to their connection with certain digestive diseases, you should check out *Grain Brain: The Surprising Truth about Wheat* by David Perlmutter and Kristen Loberg.

If you consume alcohol and/or caffeine, don't forget that they are part of your diet. I consume both in moderation, about two drinks of each every day. Caffeine seems to help me focus in the morning and recent research indicates that moderate consumption may even be beneficial.

The same seems to be true for alcohol, but keep in mind, like sugar, alcohol is also empty calories. Like some sugars such as fructose, it also needs to be metabolized by the liver. My feeling is that it works for me as part of my stress management program. Note that seven drinks at one party isn't the same as one drink a day for a week, and that too much has a negative impact.

If you feel the need to drop some weight, you need to *change* your diet rather than *go on a diet*. Consuming less food to lose weight and then returning to your previous intake will simply cause your weight to return. Having your weight bounce up and down is worse than being consistently overweight. Exercising more will help, but diet is much more important here. If you simply stop consuming high sugar foods and drinks, you will probably end up at a healthy weight as I have. (5'10" and 142 lbs.)

Finally, you should try to stay hydrated. This is something that may require a change in lifestyle. I don't go anywhere without taking a water bottle with me. When I go for my five-mile walk, I drink half a liter during the first half of the walk, and another bottle on my way back. As I visit schools, I am happy to see water fountains designed for refilling water bottles. I also see schools allowing students to have water bottles in class.

## 4. Be a Model Learner

It's important to control your own professional development. The more you know, the easier some problems will become. As principal I arrived at school at 7:00 a.m. and worked non-stop until about 4:00 p.m. at which time I usually found that most of the rest of the staff had left and that those who remained left me alone. I devoted most of the next hour to my own personal learning, which became more efficient when the Internet arrived.

I always left at 5:00 p.m. so as not to pass the point of diminishing returns. Many principals I knew worked nights and weekends. Working too long lowers the quality of your work. It also doesn't inspire your staff when they find you are sending emails at 2:00 in the morning. I also strove to be deadly efficient while doing routine chores. My proficiency with technology was key here.

This effort in self-improvement led to earning my doctorate in education at the age of 54. Since then I haven't stopped learning. As I write this at the age of 70, I am convinced that I have more expertise than ever. I like to say that I'm more hip to the field of education than I was when I was immersed in it full time.

In addition to doing guest posts for other blogs, I devote a good deal of time to my own blog where I curate the Internet and summarize books for busy educators and parents that don't have the time to read and surf that I do. In the process of putting my daily post together, I learn a great deal. It also gives me the chance to try to influence my readers to take action that I think will improve instruction for *all* children.

## 5. Get Someone Else to Do It

As a leader, you need to look for as many tasks as possible that other people can do and delegate. As you do this, fight the urge to micromanage. This will show people that you trust them. I have seen principals who assign themselves tasks that would be best left to others. They often take on clerical tasks associated with things like standardized test administration and distribution of supplies.

I've even seen one principal running the sound system in the auditorium rather than delegating the activity to the music teachers. If you are doing any routine task, you should ask yourself, "Who else can do this as well or better than I can?" Since you will always be expected to deal with emergencies, you simply can't afford to be tied down with routine tasks.

Student teachers and administrative interns should be given real work, not just busy work. In the case of the all-important state tests, for example, I always assigned the entire job to a teacher who had an interest in joining the administrative ranks.

While being efficient is important, avoid things like reading your emails when someone is talking to you. Active listening is important as it shows respect and gives you a better chance to deal with the problem at hand. Sometimes all you have to do is listen. Again, this goes back to the all-important task of forming quality relationships.

The advice here is what I followed and it allowed me to do a complex job without suffering from stress. Hardly a week goes by without my hearing that I am missed, and it isn't unusual for former students and parents to tell me that I was the best. Caring for the people you serve and taking care of yourself worked for me. Good luck in doing these things yourself.

*Answer

Tell the teacher to park behind the car and leave her car keys in the office. When the offending driver comes to the office to complain office staff can move the teacher's car. Tell the office to let the parent know you are on your way. Swing by the cafeteria and tell the staff in no uncertain terms to start serving and that you will see them later to sort out their problem. Listen to the parent's complaint. If you can fix it fast, do it. If not, tell the parent you will investigate the problem and call back later in the day. Then go be on time for your appointment with the superintendent.

# References

Gunnars, Kris. Why is Coffee Good For You? Here Are 7 Reasons, *Authority Nutrition Online,* May 25, 2017, http://bit.ly/2rIA8h3.

Perlmutter, David with Loberg, Kristen (2013). Grain Brain: The Surprising Truth about Wheat, Little, Brown and Company: New York, NY.

Taubes, Gary (2016). *The Case Against Sugar,* Random House: New York, NY.

The Nutrition Source, Alcohol: Balancing Risks and Benefits, *The Harvard School of Public Health, downloaded June 9, 2017,* http://bit.ly/2rIG6Pg.

CHAPTER **26**

# Think About How to Do It Right, Rather Than Do It Over

"The only people who never fail are those who never try."
-Ilka Chase

IN THE LATE 1970s, a former chemistry student of mine who had graduated with an engineering degree from MIT and was working in the nuclear power business revealed a slogan that he heard too often at work. The saying was: "We don't have time to do it right, but we do have time to do it over."

I was stunned. This was even before thoughts of Homer Simpson lounging at the control panel of a nuclear power plant could have come to mind. Strangely enough, it also seemed humorous at the same time and didn't make sense at first.

I soon figured it out as I went about my own work and life. The main idea is that if you want to do something better, it will most likely take more time the first time than if you continue doing it the old way, because you will be doing something different. If you are very busy, the idea of taking more time to do a task certainly won't thrill you.

The problem is inertia. In physics and in human behavior it essentially means resistance to change. Knowing there is probably a better or more efficient way to do something and not exploring it may not be a crime, but it seems somewhat criminal to me. This is especially true for educators who are dealing with the future of children.

Here is a simple example from my own experience where making the effort paid dividends: learning to type properly. When I started teaching I didn't like any of the learning materials the school had so I started creating my own. It was slow going at first, but I knew learning to type well would help me create more and better looking learning materials. With persistence and practice I was soon able to type as fast as I could compose sentences in my head.

## Be Your Own Secretary

When I became a school principal it also meant that the school secretary didn't have to transcribe my handwritten notes. This freed her up to do other things that benefited the school and ultimately the children. I expected the staff to proofread their evaluations while the school secretary proofread my correspondence.

I also embraced technology. When I was a principal back in the 1990s, I had been using spreadsheets since I published a review of the first one (VisiCalc) that was invented in 1979. As a result, it took me about half an hour to do my yearly budget while my colleagues worked nights and weekends with their yellow pads and calculators that showed only one number at a time.

I also took the time to learn how to select, sort, and display data in a powerful and more informative manner from relational databases that I had created. I've seen many people engage in what amounts to serial searches of data since learning a modest amount of coding was something they were convinced they couldn't do.

My advice, however, is not just for educators and not just aimed at the workplace. It also applies to situations where you have to do something you have never done before. Take your time analyzing a problem prior to diving in, since your first solution is not likely to be the best one you can dream up.

Changing one's behavior doesn't always take more time and the new behavior that seems better may fail to improve anything or even make things worse. You simply won't know for sure unless you take the time to try, but doing things the same way over and over is unlikely to deliver improvements.

In my life I have found the effort to constantly improve well worth it. I hope you and the people you touch can adopt this approach to work and life in general. As the actress, Ilka Chase, once said, "The only people who never fail are those who never try."

CHAPTER **27**

# As A Teacher Or Anyone Else, It's Important To Get Good At What You Don't Like To Do.

"If you get good at something you don't like you just might start liking it." -Dr. Doug Green

NO MATTER WHAT you do as part of your work, there are likely to be parts that you enjoy less than others. In their book *Designing Your Life: How to Build a Well-Lived Life*, Bill Burnett and Dave Evans advise you to get good at what you don't like to do. This will allow you to do it quickly and efficiently. If you are unskilled at these things, however, they will likely take longer and you may find that you have to do them over.

When I read this I realized that I had been following this principle ever since I started teaching in 1970. At the time I was very excited about getting my students as excited about my subject, chemistry, as I was.

On the day before the first day of school I met with the faculty and got my schedule. Much to my dismay, right in the middle of my schedule was *lunch duty*. Ouch! So I went to college for five years and earned two degrees so I could monitor a cafeteria filled with middle and high school students. That certainly wasn't the plan. I didn't see lunch duty in the course catalog.

It was then that I decided that if I had to do this job, I was going to learn how to do it well so that my time in the cafeteria would at least suck less. I quickly got to know the students who seemed the most rowdy and it wasn't long before they were behaving well for me. I simply found out what they were interested in and talked to them about it. I treated them with respect from the start and it wasn›t long before the respect was coming back. I also acted like I enjoyed being with them and it wasn't long before I did.

While improving at tasks you don't like, it's likely you will find that you dislike them less. If you're lucky, you may even start to enjoy them to some extent. For the most part, people tend to enjoy things they do well.

Another approach is to try to shift the task to someone else. Be sure to let your supervisor know which parts of your job you like and which you would rather not do. You can indicate your willingness to continue with the less likable work, but make sure the boss knows you would like to offload it if possible. Enlightened leaders want happy workers and should try to make tasks fit everyone's skills and passions as much as possible.

## If You Are the Boss

If you are a supervisor, you can look for opportunities to delegate the work you like less to others. Be careful, however, because if you delegate every task that is seen as undesirable, you will be viewed as someone who isn't willing to do their share of the dirty work. You can even look for some dirty work to take on that you don't mind too much.

As a principal, I would patrol the property prior to the start of school each day. When I did this, I always had a small plastic grocery bag in hand so I could pick up trash as I encountered it. At first I did this to keep the place neat, as neat places are more likely to stay that way while messy places attract more mess. I soon realized that I was sending a message to parents, staff, and students that I was willing to do some dirty work. Look for opportunities to do the same.

In some cases undesirable tasks present themselves to an organization. When this happens, be careful about taking them on because once you know how to do something, the job may be yours for good. In my case I made sure not to learn how to clear jams from the school's copiers that the teachers and office staff used. I knew that if I did I would be called upon frequently to do so. As I've said earlier in the book, clerical tasks are best left to the people with the best clerical skills, and they don't tend to be the administrators.

In my view the best leaders see to it that undesirable tasks are spread around. People will notice who does what and should be more motivated to do some dirty work if they see that it is fairly shared–they might even get good at it and not find it so dirty anymore.

## Reference

Burnett, Bill and Evans, Dave (2016). *Designing Your Life: How to Build a Well-Lived Life*, Alfred A. Knopf: New York, NY.

# CHAPTER 28

# A Word About Flipping Your Class

"Flipping is easier in some subjects than others, but all teachers can do it sometimes." -Jonathan Bergman

IF YOU HAVE been reading my blog or just about any modern education journal, you have no doubt run across the concept of flipping your class. This is a teaching method in which the direct instruction that a teacher would traditionally do in front of the entire class is delivered via technology.

For this to work, each student needs access to their own laptop or tablet. Programs where every student has a device are known as 1:1 programs—that is, for every one student there is one computing device. Students also need to be able to take their devices home.

I first learned about this effort by reading Jonathan Bergman and Arron Sam's 2012 book *Flip Your Classroom: Reach Every Student in Every Classroom Every Day*. The authors first recorded their lessons out of selfishness. They were spending inordinate amounts of time re-teaching lessons to students who missed class, and their recorded lectures became their first line of defense. Student feedback was positive and even some students who were in class were watching the online videos to review the content.

When the teachers realized that class time could be more effectively used to help students with concepts they didn't understand,
their *flipped classroom* was born. They used the same tests from the
previous year and found that the students scored higher.

They realized that for some students, the teacher talks too fast and
they can't keep up with notetaking. Others miss classes due to sports,
music, or illness. Some focus on a grading rubric and get good grades
without a lot of understanding. These are some of the problems a
flipped classroom can address.

## Effective Personalized Learning

When Bergman and Sams began flipping their classrooms, they
quickly realized that they had stumbled on a framework that enabled
them to effectively personalize the education of each student. When
they presented their flipped classroom model to educators around the
world, many said, "this is reproducible, scalable, customizable, and
easy for teachers to wrap their minds around."

The next breakthrough came when an exchange student who had
taken no chemistry started mid-year. As it was not possible to start
chemistry in the middle, she was told to start with the unit I videos
from the previous September. Working at her own pace she completed 80% of the course in one semester. Since she didn't go to the next
unit until she exhibited mastery, a *mastery learning* aspect entered the
program. When the authors saw this, they reasoned that all students
should do the same.

Flipped/mastery allows each student to move at his or her own
pace. The teachers put together a large pool of test items for each unit.
When students feel ready for a unit test, they take it on a computer
and view their score right away.

If they score 85% or better, they go on to the next unit. If not, they
huddle with the teacher, who looks at the items they missed and sets
up some additional learning activities. After some more effort, they
take another version of the same unit test. This process continues until
mastery is reached and they move on to the next unit.

## Some Misconceptions

In some cases the term flipped is used to imply that you flip traditional classroom direct instruction with traditional homework. Some think that videos are only watched outside of class. This shouldn't be the case. Students should be able to watch videos anywhere, anytime, including in class.

Innovative schools are even equipping their school buses with WiFi so students can watch videos during a commute. Online textbooks can also be part of the plan. Such books offer text along with interactive graphics and short video clips. They should also be effective for allowing students to advance at their own pace.

Most schools have a significant number of students who are poor and who don't have Internet access at home. As long as the school can issue a laptop and allow students to take them home, kids without Internet access can simply download the videos they want to watch next before they leave school. Not having the Internet at home might even be beneficial. Kids without it could only access content associated with their classes and would not be able to engage in recreational surfing.

## Life as a Flipped Teacher

As a flipped teacher, you don't have to go to school and perform five times a day. Instead, you spend your days interacting with and helping students. One huge benefit of flipping is that the students who struggle get the most help.

Students are responsible for making appropriate use of the resident expert to help them understand the concepts. The role of the teacher in the classroom is to help students, not to deliver information. Students also need to learn they can pause and rewind their teacher and how to take notes they can use the next day in class to get their questions answered.

Jon and Aaron found that some of their busiest students worked ahead in anticipation of missing class for other activities. But since their introduction of the flipped model, their role has changed.

They spend most of the class walking around helping the students who struggle most. This may be the single most important reason just about any student can thrive in a flipped world.

This is not to say they ignore the top students, it's just that the majority of their attention no longer goes to them. Special education teachers tend to love this model as well since students with special needs can watch the videos as many times as necessary to learn the material, and get lots of help during class. The pause button can also break up the lesson into briefer segments so students can learn on their own schedule. A few students even watch videos at faster speeds.

With the traditional model, students returning from an illness were likely to face a great deal of confusion due to the fact that they missed material. With the flipped system, students can, not only watch videos at home if they aren't too sick, they can simply pick up where they left off when they return to school.

Perhaps most importantly, flipping allows teachers to build better relationships with students. This is due to the increased teacher–student interaction. Because they no longer just stand and talk at kids, many of their classroom discipline problems evaporate. As I stated in an earlier chapter, building strong working relationships with all students is the most important thing that teachers can do.

## Videos - Make or Find

If you plan to try flipping, only make videos for your students if it is the most appropriate thing to do. Consider using someone else's videos to save time, or if you aren't good at making your own. You can even have your students help you search for and make videos. There are lots of free videos online and you can buy the ones the authors use if you teach chemistry. Note, however, that your students might enjoy seeing you in at least some of the videos.

The authors use Camtasia Studio but there are lots of options. You may want to draw on the screen with a pen. You can do so with a separate tablet or just use an interactive whiteboard. They include a chapter that contains lots of tips for making videos students will love. Your tech department can help you make the videos available online. Some teachers also burn DVDs to use in places where the Internet isn't available.

The length of the videos you make or select should depend on your students' age. One recommendation I've seen suggests you keep the length to two times the grade level. That would be eight minute videos for fourth graders, for example. Putting an entire course of videos together will take time unless you purchase an off-the-shelf course. It might also be better to try one unit as a test run before you flip it all.

## Mastery Learning Isn't a New Idea

The idea of mastery learning entered the profession in the 1960s and 1970s. Few teachers used it, however, because it is difficult to teach and monitor a room full of students learning different things at the same time. Flipping can make mastery learning much easier, as each student can watch the videos appropriate for their current understanding.

Assessment can be done with a bank of exams online or by using traditional testing methods. Students take the test they are supposedly ready for and if they don't demonstrate mastery, the teacher can provide remediation prior to taking another form of the assessment.

The teacher checks with each student daily and organizes groups who need to work on the same topic or do the same lab activity. To do this, teachers also must be comfortable letting students control their learning to a greater extent. It shouldn't be too difficult spotting students who are slacking, however, as they will soon fall behind.

The flipped approach can work in most subjects. Even physical education teachers can use the idea. In their case, kids can learn the activity by watching a video so when they arrive at class they can get moving right away rather than standing around while the teacher explains what to do.

Flipping can also facilitate project-based learning, which allows students to control some of the content. You might find that first year foreign language students spend more time speaking in the target language during class.

## Differentiation Becomes Possible

The flipped mastery approach turns out to be an easy way to differentiate and personalize the classroom for *all* students. In the traditional classroom this is very difficult. But in this case, students take assessments they are ready for and don't move on until they demonstrate understanding. This should prevent frustration.

The classroom becomes a learning space and the focus is no longer on the teacher. Just getting by no longer happens. You can use the term level rather than unit to make it seem like a game where you unlock the next level. The students who like the sit- and- get form of delivery will usually come around, and some students will start bugging other teachers to flip.

The authors suggest that you expect three years for your flipped mastery model to become part of the school culture. Year one is the most difficult, and year two is when you work out the remaining bugs.

Don't make the mistake of starting with all students moving at the same pace and then switching to the mastery model. This causes needless confusion for students. Make sure you educate parents at the start. Watch a few videos with the students, using the pause and rewind buttons. Also teach note-taking techniques.

Expect each student to ask at least one question per video. Such questions can help you improve the videos. If you have a SMART Board, use it as a station that students can use. Other stations can allow for individual or group work and hands-on activities like science labs.

## Assessment and Grading Issues

Be sure to let students take all assessments, including the final if you have one on their own schedule. You should find a lot of students helping each other. Teachers can form groups working on the same topic but don't be surprised if groups spontaneously form. Formative assessment happens daily as students demonstrate their understanding.

Some teachers require 75% scores on summative assessments before students go on, but even students that score 75% or better can be allowed to retake tests for better grades. Computer-based testing with a system that constructs unique tests from banks of questions for each objective as needed can control cheating.

The authors use Moodle and find text item construction to be an ongoing activity. If report card grades are still required by the school you can use the summative assessment grades and the number of units mastered to put a grade together. The authors base 50% on summative assessment scores and 50% on how many units the student has completed.

Students who complete all units with time to spare can start another course if your school allows it. If not, they can go deeper into the subject's content and come up with their own open-ended projects. This means that they can control the content they encounter, which is seldom the case for traditional courses like chemistry.

Students who don't finish all units can keep on going at the end of the school year or finish in summer school if you have one. Instead of starting from the beginning again next year, they can simply *finish* when they finish, just like the runners in a race. This makes so much sense to me.

Some innovative schools are replacing traditional grades with things like badges and/or portfolios. You would get the course badge when you complete the final unit. Your transcript would indicate which badges you have earned and how long each one took. To get into an elite school you would need lots of badges, badges completed quickly, and badges in challenging courses.

## Conclusion

As I travel around and visit schools, I find that most high schools feature at least some teachers who are experimenting with some version of flipping. If I were teaching chemistry today, as I did from 1971 to 1982, I would certainly start flipping. To me flipping with mastery is our best hope for reforming education in order to benefit students rather than to generate useless test scores. Good luck with your flipping efforts.

## Reference

Bergman, Jonathan and Sams, Arron (2012). *Flip Your Classroom: Reach Every Student in Every Classroom Every Day*, International Society for Technology in Education: Washington, D.C.

CHAPTER **29**

# Can We Save Opera? The Barriers to Digging the World's Greatest Art Form

"If you are not currently an opera fan, *it's not too late!*" -Dr. Doug Green

THIS CHAPTER MAY not seem like it belongs here, but it is my hope that I can somehow help save what I see as the world's most amazing art form, which seems to be fading as most of its fans age.

As a principal of a school with 90% in poverty and 25% refugees, I brought in the local opera company every year to do assemblies (Tri-Cities Opera, Binghamton, New York). Their shows were very big hits with the students. Part of the reason, I think, is that my kids weren't jaded yet. They were exposed to other music, but no one told them that opera wasn't cool.

As an opera lover, I go to performances whenever I can and, un-fortunately, the typical crowd appears to have a median age greater than my 70 years. We need to fix that, because it is easy to make the case that opera is the greatest art form humans have ever invented. It usually features the best orchestras, the best singers, very interesting sets, and excellent costumes and lighting. Sometimes there is even some top dancing.

So if it is so good, why don't more people dig it? I think there are four reasons. The first is that it features classical music. It is not your current popular tunes for the most part. It is the type of orchestral music that was big prior to the time when we all had radio, TV and popular music.

I was a college student in the late '60s. By the time my senior year rolled around, I had a few credits to play with so I took a music appreciation course. It was essentially a name-that-tune course featuring the greatest hits of classical music. Even though I wasn't a classical fan at the time, I knew that this music had to be good or it wouldn't be "classical." Something simply doesn't last if it isn't good or great. For some reason, I knew that this stuff was an acquired taste and worth some effort.

Once you enjoy classical orchestra music, the next barrier is what opera does to the human voice. Operas tend to push the envelope of what the human voice can do much more than popular singing. Only the best singers can handle the opera parts. Since most people don't hear this type of singing and can't sing like this, their ears don't get accustomed to it. As an acquired taste, most people have to listen to it for a while before they can appreciate it.

## Opera's Greatest Hits

Some opera singing is easier to appreciate than others for people just getting started. There are starter operas, which are easier for beginners, and there are operas that you should stay away from at first. Puccini is a good place to start since a lot of his work has been taken to Broadway in one form or another. The musical "Rent" is essentially Puccini's "La Boheme" and you can hear a number of Puccini's themes in works by Andrew Lloyd Weber and others. Some works by Mozart, Verdi, Bizet, and Rossini are also easy to appreciate. I would avoid Wagner and Richard Strauss at first but don't rule them out later on; they are among the best.

The third barrier, especially for guys, are the plots. They tend to be something you could summarize in a Tweet. They are essentially the "chick flicks" of the music world. By that I mean no offense to women, but they are not exactly full of action. There is lots of love and outfits and furniture, but not a lot of what many men look for in movies. It's kind of anti-James Bond. As I watched a lot of girly movies while my wife was suffering from ALS (Lou Gehrig's Disease), I have become more tolerant of plots where not a lot happens. For me, the music and the singing makes up for it and I don't have to spend much time figuring out a tricky plot.

Finally, there is the language. Most operas are not done in English. There are some more modern works that were written in English, and there are English translations for many standards. You can read English translations on the back of your seat or over the stage to keep track of the plot, but it is usually summarized in your program. Listening to Italian, French, or German is a bit like listening to Celtic music in Gaelic so go for it.

## Length and Price and Don't Expect the Ladies to Be Fat

When I shared this article with some friends, they mentioned length and price as possible barriers. The cost of an opera is usually similar to the cost of a musical. You can pay a lot or a little depending on your seat and the location of the opera. As for length, operas do tend to run longer than musicals and some run a lot longer. With a single intermission of half an hour, the typical opera runs about three and a half hours. Some, however, can last beyond five hours with two intermissions so try to check that out before you commit. The way I look at it is that you get more for your money at an opera.

As for the cliché that says "an opera isn't over until the fat lady sings," that hardly describes reality. Any female lead will sing many times during a single opera, and while some of them are on the large side of average, very few would be considered obese. The typical opera singer is more likely to be relatively slender and attractive. In a way,

157

opera singers are like athletes. They need to be able to move grace-fully and look good in their costumes. My favorite opera women are Rene Fleming and Anna Netrebko, who are anything but fat ladies.

If you aren't into opera yet, there is still time as long as you are generating carbon dioxide. If you have children or grandchildren, take them to an opera if you can. They won't know that it isn't cool and in the process they may just begin to realize that it is indeed the greatest art form humans have ever created. You also may help the audience become a bit less gray and ensure that it won't fade away.

CHAPTER **30**

# Epilogue

WHEN I TALK about fixing education, I don't want to imply that there was a time in the past when it wasn't broken. I see it as being broken from the beginning when the first 19th century schools were modeled after the factories that employed parents. The one-size-fits-all approach that is still common today, was essentially established because it made teaching easy for the adults.

It's clear to me that what we need are reforms that allow for individualized self-paced learning. Instead, the current reforms require teachers to prepare their entire class to take the same test at the same time based the birth dates of their students. We have this due to pressure from the corporate class to come up with "objective" scores that can be used to judge students, teachers, and schools.

There is also an expectation that schools will somehow close the achievement gaps between arbitrarily chosen subgroups. This is due in part tq pressure from minority groups who don't like the fact that Black and Hispanic students score worse on the tests. It's clear to me that the gaps are due to poverty rather than race or ethnicity as the lower scoring groups are more likely to be poor, and being poor is stressful for many reasons.

The big stress as far as test scores go is caused by the fact that in poor homes, students are usually exposed to less language. As a result they show up to school already behind and they usually stay behind.

The one-size-fits all approach exposes them to the same things that the more advanced kids get, for which they most likely are not developmentally ready.

The irony about achievement gaps is that they will only grow if every student learns at their own pace. The faster learners will learn faster than their less able classmates. The only way to close the gaps, therefore, is to slow down the faster learners. Unfortunately, many schools do this rather well. You can also narrow gaps thanks to the ceiling effect, as any student who is already near the top score has nowhere to go but down.

The premise that all students should achieve at some arbitrary level is fallacious. The idea that you can put a number on each student like you could weigh a pig is equally fallacious. Unfortunately, these two things are the cornerstones of modern reform.

Although test scores have an objective look, the process of putting tests together is subjective. It's time to realize the evaluating students and teachers needs to have a subjective aspect. Teachers with expertise can evaluate student projects that don't lend themselves to percentage scores. For objectivity, they can count the number of units and courses a student finishes in a flipped/mastery classroom.

Administrators with expertise can tell if a teacher has respectful relationships with students. They can tell if the students are engaged in learning or are off task. They can tell if the teacher is doing a decent job of checking for understanding. They can tell if a teacher is trying to differentiate the learning. They can also count the number of discipline referrals from each teacher.

If necessary, you can list scores for such items, but such scores will be derived from subjective judgments. If subjective scoring works for figure skating, diving, and even boxing, it can work for evaluating teachers and students.

Finally, I return to the title of this book. Teaching and learning are among the most complex things humans do. As a society we need to recognize this and hold education in appropriate esteem. While this book takes educators to task, I should note that I have great respect for anyone who enters this profession.

One thing we also know is that the nature of employment that schools prepare students for is changing. It's hard to say what kind of jobs will be available at a given date in the future, but some trends are clear. Many jobs are being automated and performed by robots or computers. For this reason, teachers should promote engagement in project work with an emphasis on creativity. For a list of jobs that are disappearing and what to do about it see my blog post on the topic at http://bit.ly/2A23Djm.

I fear that current reforms are pushing people out and giving others no good reason to get in. I hope that efforts such as mine and the many other education experts who join me have come in time to turn things around and fix at least some of what needs to be fixed. Please join me in this vital fight.

CHAPTER **31**

# Books You Should Find in Your Professional Development Library and Links to My Summaries

WHEN I STARTED my blog at DrDougGreen.com in 2009, a key feature was my book summaries. I started summarizing books when I was doing my doctoral work. My summaries helped me internalize the book's key concepts so that when class discussions took place, I was up to speed on the issues. I was also the only student at the time (1992-1995) who brought a laptop to class. It was an early Apple laptop with a whopping six megabytes of RAM. This meant that I could have Word and Excel open at the same time!

At some point I shared my summaries with my administrative colleagues and they loved them. I still use them myself when I need to review the concepts from a book. My secondary goal is to promote sales of books that I feel are important for educators to know about.

While I'm always on the lookout for hot education books, I don't limit myself to the genre. Throughout this book I have taken issue with the corporate class for their push to test and punish schools and teachers. That doesn't mean, however, that educators can't learn from how businesses operate. We shouldn't try to measure the abilities of students like businesses count quarterly sales, but we can learn from some of what business does.

As of this writing there are no less than 145 book summaries on my blog. Any school could put all of them in their professional development library for about $3,000. I'm sure many superintendents could find this amount in their budget without much trouble. Some schools, however, would have to take a few years to afford them all.

The rest of this chapter contains nutshell descriptions of the forty-one books that I recommend you purchase first if you can't afford them all. I have also included a link to my summary for each book. After the nutshells, there is a list of these books sorted by author that you can give to your librarian and ask that person to put a purchase order together so you can buy these books now. Happy reading.

## The Book Thumbnails: Sorted By Title With Links To My Summaries

*Ball or Bands: Football vs Music as an Educational and Community Investment* by John Gerdy uses research to support the notion that due to costs, injuries, its focus on elite male athletes, and a negative impact on school cultures, support for high school football can no longer be defended. He also makes a case for why music and the arts in general need more support. He comes at this topic as a musician and an athlete with a brief career in the NBA. Be strong if you decide to take on *king football*. http://bit.ly/1HpM2iT

*Better By Mistake – Improve your life and performance* by Alina Tugend features the big idea that embracing mistakes can make us happier and more productive in every facet of our lives. It examines the tension between the idea that we must make mistakes to learn, and the fact that we often get punished for them. It points out the fact that educators should design lessons so that students feel safe enough to take risks and learn from their mistakes. http://bit.ly/2t2gFsq

*Better Than College: How to Build a Better Life Without a Four-Year Degree* by Blake Boles offers the thesis that you can skip four-year college and still get a higher education. This may seem nuts, but spend a few moments considering the propositions, and you'll begin to see why Zero Tuition College (ZTC) holds just as much life-changing potential as traditional college. http://bit.ly/1UxwopQ

*Blogging for Educators: Writing for Professional Learning* by Starr Sackstein provides a strong rationale for why educators should blog, along with advice on how to get started. She is one of the best education bloggers I have found to date, and I explore the educational blogosphere every day. http://bit.ly/1wTT63I

*Brain Rules: 12 Principles for Surviving and Thriving at Work, Home, and School* by John Medina tells how what we know about brain science can be used to positively influence our daily lives. This book is vital for educators, policy makers, and anyone who wants to get more out of their gray matter. http://bit.ly/1gfQ4tH

*Catching Up or Leading the Way: American Education in the Age of Globalization* by Yong Zhao tells the story of how China seems to want an education that America seems eager to throw away. This is one that respects individual talents, supports divergent thinking, tolerates deviation, and encourages creativity. At the same time, the U.S. government is pushing for the kind of education that China is moving away from. This is one that features standardization of curricula and an emphasis on preparing students for standardized tests. He wonders why Americans who hold individual rights in high regard would let the government dictate what children should learn, when they should learn it, and how they are evaluated. http://bit.ly/1uhFyMX

*Counting What Counts: Reframing Education Outcomes* by Yong Zhao and friends takes on the current system with its focus on standardized tests and their sole focus on cognitive skills. Chapters are devoted to defining a variety of non-cognitive skills that are connected with success in life and the current status of how to assess them. They make a case for a new paradigm that would move the system toward more personalized learning and assessment with more focus on non-cognitive skills. http://bit.ly/2pIfYjq

*Creating Innovators: The Making of Young People Who Will Change the World* by Tony Wagner explores what parents, teachers, and employers must do to develop the capacities of young people to become innovators. Tony profiles innovators to identify patterns in their childhood that made them what they are. He shows how to apply his findings to education and tells parents how to compensate for poor schools. Keys include collaboration, interdisciplinary problem-solving, and intrinsic motivation. Sixty original videos are included that you can access via a smartphone. Go to Creating Innovators for a trailer. http://bit.ly/2t2QNNm

*Creative Schools: The Grassroots Revolution That's Transforming Education* by Sir Ken Robinson and Lou Aronica offers advice for educators and policy makers that can bring rigorous, personalized, and engaged education to everyone. As a leading voice in education, it's vital that anyone interested hear what Sir Ken has to say. If you haven't seen his number one TED Talk check that out too. http://bit.ly/1dvUdNm

*Discipline Survival Guide for the Secondary Teacher, 2nd Ed*, by Julia Thompson takes on what may be the most unpleasant part of the profession and a top reason why teachers leave. She draws on up-to-date research and theory that can help students become more self-disciplined, goal-oriented, and successful learners as teachers enhance leadership skills. She focuses on student motivation, classroom management, relationships, instructional techniques, safety, and high expectations. This 350 page effort is easy to read and can be used as a desktop reference. My summary contains key ideas, but there is a lot more I left out. Every student teacher, beginning teacher, and veteran teacher with disciplinary problems should have this at their side.

There is lots of advice for parents too. As a former secondary teacher and elementary principal, I can assure you, most of this applies to students of all ages. http://bit.ly/2t2uMxP

*Ditch That Textbook* by Matt Miller starts in 2007 when he was lecturing and teaching from a textbook. He knew the kids were bored and so was he. He was stuck in the old paradigm of using the textbook as the curriculum, along with worksheets and multiple choice tests. While I'm always leery of words as acronyms as their authors usually have to stretch things a bit to make them work, the DITCH acronym really does work. It stands for Different, Innovative, Tech-Laden, Creative, and Hands-On. These are the hallmarks of Matt's model that he rolls out in this book. In addition to ditching your textbook, this model also requires you to ditch your curriculum and, perhaps more importantly, ditch your mindset. http://bit.ly/1PTCVW0

*Drive: The Surprising Truth About What Motivates Us* by Daniel Pink is a must-read for educators and parents alike. Dan summarizes current research and does a great job turning it into interesting and understandable prose that educators can apply to their practice. http://bit.ly/2durY4s

*Driven by Data: A Practical Guide to Improve Instruction* by Paul Bambrick-Santoyo offers a step by step approach to preparing your students for high-stakes tests while students work to master standards. While you may be hoping for the current testing madness to end, Paul offers a practical way for your school to out-perform other schools with similar demographics while the current tests are still with us. Part two includes specific workshop activities for data leaders. http://bit.ly/1qwnsPn

*The Element: How Finding Your Passion Changes Everything* by Sir Ken Robinson deals with the point where natural talent meets personal passion. Ken explores the conditions that lead us to live lives filled with passion, confidence, and personal achievement. The stories about people from a wide variety of fields entertain and inspire.

The book is a classic. If you read it a while ago, my summary will be a good review. Also check out Sir Ken's TED Talks. http://bit.ly/2qdRbqV

*Flip Your Classroom: Reach Every Student in Every Classroom Every Day* by Jonathan Bergmann and Arron Sams is a must read for anyone interested in flipping their classroom. It provides a window into a flipped classroom led by two educators who were driven by a simple question: What is best for the students in my classroom? This book chronicles their journey from their first shaky steps at trying to *flip* their classrooms to their current *best practice so far,* the flipped-mastery classroom model. Learn from their mistakes so that you can make new mistakes, and then share what you've learned to improve the model for all. Learn how flipping produces better test results and better learning. Also learn how it will allow you to interact more often with your students and develop more personal relationships. http://bit.ly/1atBiOe

*Finnish Lessons 2.0: What Can the World Learn from Educational Change in Finland* by Pasi Sahlberg Teachers College Press: New York, NY is the story of Finland's extraordinary reforms and one that should inform policymakers and educators around the world, most of whom are on the wrong track. Sahlberg has lived and studied these reforms for decades and is a clever and engaging storyteller. Just because the Finnish demographic is different from that in the U.S., it doesn't mean that we can't copy some of what they have done. http://bit.ly/IHpyNv

*Girls and Sex: Navigating the Complicated New Landscape* by Peggy Orenstein tells the real story of what it's like being a girl from middle school to college in today's highly sexualized climate. Peggy scoured current research and had in-depth interviews with over seventy high school and college girls to compile this gripping and sometimes discouraging story. I first listened to the book on Audible prior to buying the physical book for this summary. http://bit.ly/2hEyWDC

*Hacking Assessment: 10 Ways To Go Gradeless In a Traditional Grades School* by Starr Sackstein - When she started her new system, Starr found that her lower-level students liked the idea of not being judged, as they lacked success with the traditional system. Rather than being assigned additional nightly homework, students just continue working on the projects they are working on in class. Top students had to realize that top grades had little to do with learning and were more about their need to feel smart. Portfolios of work are key here and you can make YouTube videos to display student work. When grades are required, you can let the students work with you to determine grades together. More important is the ongoing feedback from the teacher and fellow students. http://bit.ly/1UPaygh

*How We Learn: The Surprising Truth About When, Where, and Why It Happens* by Benedict Carey summarizes research on this topic, much of which educators have yet to implement. Education's leaders need to read this book and work to reform the system accordingly. http://bit.ly/1pTWwda

*Inevitable: Mass Customized Learning in the Age of Empowerment* by Charles Schwahn & Beatrice McGarvey shares an exciting vision for education that uses today's powerful mass customizing technology to meet the individual learning needs and interests of every learner every day. The goal is to do for learners what Apple does for music lovers, Amazon does for readers, and what Google does for seekers of information. Mass Customized Learning is necessary and doable. http://bit.ly/2sxXTpe

*The Innovator's Mindset: Empower Learning, Unleash Talent, and Lead a Culture of Creativity* by George Couros gives great encouragement and advice to teachers seeking to improve continuously in the face of budget restrictions, policies that don't make sense, and curricula that are way too static for a constantly changing world. This would be a great book to give to every teacher in your school. http://bit.ly/2aU9yZV

*Intelligence and How to Get It: Why Schools and Cultures Count* by Richard Nisbett shows how intelligence is mostly determined by one's environment and provides concrete things that parents and teachers can do to make kids smarter. He is convinced that intelligence has nothing to do with race and lots to do with hard work. This is a must read for educators and parents alike. http://bit.ly/1HTZ9Y0

*Mathematical Mindsets: Unleashing Students' Potential Through Creative Math, Inspiring Messages, and Innovative Teaching* by Jo Boaler with Foreword by Carol Dweck starts with the premise that math is the subject most in need of a makeover. Jo draws on modern brain research to show how changes in teaching and parenting can change students' mathematical pathways. http://bit.ly/1V8dt3k

*(The) Medici Effect: What Elephants and Epidemics Can Teach Us About Innovation* by Frans Johansson considers breakthrough insights at the intersection of ideas, concepts, and cultures. He recommends that you expose yourself to a range of cultures, learn differently, reverse your assumptions, and take on multiple perspectives. The tips on brainstorming research are worth the price alone. Although this book was published in 2004 by Harvard Business School Press, it is just as current today as when it was written. Johansson is a writer and consultant who lives in New York City. http://bit.ly/2tpohpn

*Mindset: The New Psychology of Success – How We Can Learn to Fulfill Our Potential* by Carol S. Dweck, Ph.D. will help you learn how a simple belief about yourself guides a large part of your life. That belief relates to the fact that we now understand that the brain can grow new connections and learn. It means that teachers must constantly emphasize the notion with their students that intelligence isn't a fixed commodity. It is vital that all teachers and parents read this book. http://bit.ly/2hbNrPs

*(The) Myths of Standardized Tests: Why They Don't Tell You What You Think They Do* by Phillip Harris, Bruce M. Smith, and Joan Harris (with a little help from ten of their friends) provides great ammunition for anyone who wants to join the fight against the test and punish reforms that schools and students are currently suffering from. http://bit.ly/1Nunc0C

*(The) No Asshole Rule: Building a Civilized Workplace and Surviving One That Isn't* by Robert I. Sutton should help organizations of all kinds make their cultures less toxic and more productive. Click at the bottom of any page to get a copy so you can get started dealing with jerky behavior where you live and work. http://bit.ly/1Qt9UCC

*On Your Mark: Challenging the Conventions of Grading and Reporting* by Thomas R. Guskey explains to all teachers why their grading practices are probably wrong for many reasons. If you teach or know teachers you need to share this book.

*Preparing Students for a Project-Based World* by Bonnie Lathram, Bob Lenz, and Tom Vander Ark spells out the rationale for introducing project-based learning as an excellent way to prepare students for college and careers. It is the first of three reports about the new economy and inequities in student preparation. The next two parts will deal with preparing teachers and students for a project-based classroom. http://bit.ly/2dKDV8N.

*QUIET: The Power of Introverts In a World That Can't Stop Talking* by Susan Cain tells the story of how being introverted has its advantages and how the extrovert ideal is overrated. Learn how forced collaboration can stand in the way of innovation, and how the leadership potential of introverts is often overlooked. This book is passionately argued and draws on cutting-edge research in psychology and neuroscience. Leaders, educators, and parents need to pay attention to Cain's findings. Also check Susan's TED talk. http://bit.ly/1MxNuzQ

*Readicide: How Schools Are Killing Reading and What You Can Do About It* by Kelly Gallagher explains how most schools teach reading in a way that kills most students' love of reading. It also gives advice for how to fix the problem. Educators at the middle school and elementary levels along with parents should read this. http://bit.ly/2tkRjGn

*Rethinking Value-Added Models in Education: Critical Perspective on Tests and Assessment-Based Accountability* by Audrey

Amrein-Beardsley describes and analyzes the imposition of value added test-based evaluation of teachers, the theory behind it, the real-life consequences, and its fundamental flaws. It contains great detail and should be in the hands of any person or organization fighting this alarming practice. http://bit.ly/1zaiI6Y .

*Sexting Panic: Rethinking Criminalization, Privacy, and Consent* by Amy Adele Hasinoff takes on common wisdom and shows how it is harmful to many girls since it lets privacy violators off the hook. It sees sexting as a natural part of the process of developing a normal and healthy sex life and promotes the idea of explicit consent when it comes to distributing private media images. This book belongs in every school and in the hands of every teen parent and policy maker. http://bit.ly/1qfEatc

*Smart Strengths: Building Character, Resilience, and Relationships in Youth* by John M. Yeager, Sherri W. Fisher, and David Shearon introduces the SMART model for changing a school one person at a time. It's about bringing positive education to students and maximizing the students' inherent strengths to foster character and achievement. It is research-supported and loaded with activities, resources, and real-life examples. Any school looking to improve should seriously consider the advice in this important book. http://bit.ly/2tkMs88

*Special Education 2.0: Breaking Taboos to Build a NEW Education Law* by Miriam Kurtzig Freedman points out the successes and flaws of the 1975 law that established federal control of public school special education programs. It argues against labeling students and for giving *all* students what they need without wasting money on bureaucracy and litigation. Share this with policy makers you know. http://bit.ly/2pqZVa2

*Teaching Outside the Lines: Developing Creativity in Every Learner* by Doug Johnson encourages teachers to believe that all students can be creative and gives specific advice for how to foster it in schools. http://bit.ly/2tkOHZ6

# TEACHING ISN'T ROCKET SCIENCE, IT'S WAY MORE COMPLEX

*Teaching with Poverty in Mind: What Being Poor Does to Kids' Brains and What Schools Can Do About It* by Eric Jensen explains how the stresses encountered by poor students can impact their achievement in school and what schools can do about it. http://bit.ly/2f5BppN

*The Test: Why Our Schools Are Obsessed with Standardized Testing – But You Don't Have to Be* by Anya Kamenetz explains in some detail the ten things wrong with state tests along with some history and politics. She goes on to tell educators and parents what they should do to help kids survive the madness. Anyone who dislikes state tests should get this book. http://bit.ly/2404105

*Test-and-Punish: How the Texas Education Model Gave America Accountability Without Equity* by John Kuhn follows the history of the modern education reform movement from its roots in Texas. While the tone is strongly one-sided, John makes a compelling case for reforms that diagnose-and-support and finds a way to finance schools in a more equitable manner. If you haven't joined his battle, it may be time. http://bit.ly/1scvmEQ

*Thinking Fast and Slow: How Your Brain Works* by Noble Prize winner Daniel Kahneman takes us on a ground-breaking tour of the mind and explains the two systems that drive the way we think. The *fast* system is intuitive and emotional. The *slow* system is more deliberative and more logical. This highly anticipated book can help you better understand your own thinking and make better decisions. http://bit.ly/1C0NDEm

*What Works May Hurt: Side Effects in Education* by Yong Zhao provides an important lesson that education needs to borrow from medicine. That is the study of side effects. Educational research tends to focus only on proving the effectiveness of practices and policies in pursuit of *what works*. It has generally ignored the potential harms. This article presents evidence that shows side effects are inseparable from effects. Unlike all of the other resources listed here, this is an article from a journal and not a book. Download the pdf here. http://bit.ly/2tvRJtD

# References Sorted by Author

Amrein-Beardsley, Audrey (2014). *Rethinking Value-Added Models in Education: Critical Perspective on Tests and Assessment-Based Accountability*, Routledge: New York, NY.

Bambrick-Santoyo, Paul (2010). *Driven by Data: A Practical Guide to Improve Instruction*, Jossey-Bass: San Francisco, CA.

Boaler, Jo (2016). *Mathematical Mindsets: Unleashing Students' Potential Through Creative Math, Inspiring Messages and Innovative Teaching*, Jossey-Bass: San Francisco, CA.

Boles, Blake (2012). *Better Than College: How to Build a Better Life Without a Four-Year Degree*, Tells Peak Press: Loon Lake, CA.

Boaler, Jo (2016) *Mathematical Mindsets: Unleashing Students' Potential Through Creative Math, Inspiring Messages and Innovative Teaching*, Jossey-Bass: SanFrancisco, CA.

Cain, Susan (2012). *QUIET: The Power of Introverts In a World That Can't Stop Talking,* Crown Publishers: New York, NY.

Carey, Benedict (2014). *How We Learn: The Surprising Truth About When, Where, and Why It Happens*, Random House: New York, NY.

Couros, George (2015).*The Innovator's Mindset: Empower Learning, Unleash Talent, and Lead a Culture of Creativity*, Dave Burgess Consulting: San Diego, CA.

Dweck Carol (2016) *Mindset: The New Psychology of Success – How We Can Learn to Fulfill Our Potential* , Ballentine Books: New York, NY.

Freedman, Miriam Kurtzig (2017). *Special Education 2.0: Breaking Taboos to Build a NEW Education Law,* School Law Pro: Palo Alto, CA.

Gallagher, Kelly (2009). *Readicide: How Schools Are Killing Reading and What You Can Do About It,* Stenhouse Publishers: Portland, ME)

Gerdy, John (2014). *Ball or Bands: Football vs Music as an Educational and Community Investment,* Archway Publishing: Bloomington, IN.

Guskey, Thomas R. (2015). *On Your Mark: Challenging the Conventions of Grading and Reporting,* Solution Tree Press: Bloomington, IN.

Hasinoff, Adele (2015). *Sexting Panic: Rethinking Criminalization, Privacy, and Consent,* University of Illinois Press: Urbana, IL.

Harris, Phillip, Smith, Bruce M., and Harris Joan (2011). *The Myths of Standardized Tests: Why They Don't Tell You What You Think They Do,* Rowman and Littlefeild: Lanham, MD.

Jensen, Eric (2009). *Teaching with Poverty in Mind: What Being Poor Does to Kids' Brains and What Schools Can Do About It,* ASCD: Alexandria, VA.

Johanson, Frans (2017). *The Medici Effect: What Elephants and Epidemics Can Teach Us About Innovation,* Harvard Business Review Press: Boston, MA.

Johnson, Doug (2015). *Teaching Outside the Lines: Developing Creativity in Every Learner,* Corwin: Thousand Oaks, CA.

Kamenetz, Anya (2015). *The Test: Why Our Schools Are Obsessed with Standardized Testing – But You Don't Have to Be,* Public Affairs: New York, NY.

Kahneman, Daniel (2011). *Thinking Fast and Slow: How Your Brain Works,* Farrar, Straus, and Giroux books: New York, NY.

Kuhn, John (2013). *Test-and-Punish: How the Texas Education Model Gave America Accountability Without Equity*, Park Place Publications: Austin, TX.

Lathram, Bonnie, Lenz Bob, & VanderArk, Tom (2013). *Preparing Students for a Project-Based World,* Corwin: Thousand Oaks, CA.

Medina, John (2014). *Brain Rules: 12 Principles for Surviving and Thriving at Work, Home, and School*, Pear Press: Seattle, WA.

Miller, Matt (2015). *Ditch That Textbook,* Dave Burgess Consulting, Inc: San Diego, CA.

Nisbett, Richard (2009). *Intelligence and How to Get It: Why Schools and Cultures Count* by Richard Nisbett, W. W. Norton & Company, Inc: New York, NY.

Orenstein, Peggy (2017). *Girls and Sex: Navigating the Complicated New Landscape*, Harper Collins: New York, NY.

Pink, Daniel (2011). *Drive: The Surprising Truth About What Motivates Us*, Riverhead Books: New York, NY.

Robinson, Ken (2009). *The Element: How Finding Your Passion Changes Everything,* Penguin Books: New York, NY.

Robinson, Ken and Aronica, Lou (2015). *Creative Schools: The Grassroots Revolution That's Transforming Education*, Penguin Books: New York, NY.

Sackstein, Starr (2015). *Blogging for Educators: Writing for Professional Learning*, Corwin Press: Thousand Oaks, CA.

Sackstein, Starr (2015). *Hacking Assessment: 10 Ways to Go Gradeless in a Traditional Grades School*, Times 10 Publications: Cleveland, OH.

Sahlberg, Pasi (2015). *Finnish Lessons 2.0: What Can the World Learn from Educational Change in Finland,* Teachers College Press: New York, NY.

Schwahn, Charles & McGarvey, Beatrice (2012). *Inevitable: Mass Customized Learning in the Age of Empowerment,* Chuck Schwahn and Bea McGarvey.

Sutton, Robert I. (2010). *The No Asshole Rule: Building a Civilized Workplace and Surviving One That Isn't,* Business Plus: New York, NY.

Thompson, Julia (2011). *Discipline Survival Guide for the Secondary Teacher, 2nd Ed,* Jossey-Bass: San Francisco, CA.

Tugend, Alina (2011). *Better By Mistake: Improve Your Life and Performance,* Riverside Books: New York, NY.

Wagner, Tony (2012). *Creating Innovators: The Making of Young People Who Will Change the World,* Scribner: New York, NY.

Yeager, John M., Fisher, Sherri W., & Shearon, David (2011). *Smart Strengths: Building Character, Resilience, and Relationships in Youth,* Kravis Publishing: Putnam Valley, NY.

Zhao, Youg (2009). *Catching Up or Leading the Way: American Education in the Age of Globalization,* ASCD: Alexandria, VA.

Zhao, Youg (2016). *Counting What Counts: Reframing Education Outcomes,* Solution Tree Press: Bloomington, IN.

Zhao, Youg. *What works may hurt: Side effects in education* Journal of Educational Change, ISSN 1389-2843, J Educ Change, DOI 10.1007/s10833-016-9294-4.

CPSIA information can be obtained
at www.ICGtesting.com
Printed in the USA
BVHW01s1213040118
504316BV00002B/161/P